*The Rabbit
on the Face of
the Moon*

The Rabbit on the Face of the Moon

Mythology in the Mesoamerican Tradition

Alfredo López Austin

Translated by Bernard R. Ortiz de Montellano
and Thelma Ortiz de Montellano

UNIVERSITY OF UTAH PRESS
Salt Lake City

∞ Printed on acid-free paper

Library of Congress Cataloging-in-Publication Data

López–Austin, Alfredo.
  The rabbit on the face of the moon : mythology in the mesoameri-
can tradition / Alfredo López-Austin ; translated by Bernard R. Ortiz
de Montellano and Thelma Ortiz de Montellano.
      p.   cm.
  A collection of essays that originally appeared in various issues of
México ingígena and Ojarascas.
  Includes bibliographical references and index.
    ISBN 0-87480-521-X (cloth : alk. paper). —ISBN 0-87480-527-9
(pbk. : alk. paper)
    1. Indian mythology—Mexico.   2. Indian mythology—Central
America.   3. Indians of Mexico—Folklore.   4. Indians of Central
America—Folklore.   I. Title.
F1219.3.R38L716   1996
299'.72—dc20   96-26928

Contents

Illustrations

Introduction
In the Beginning, the Flood

A wise man, Utanapishtim, lived in Shuruppak, on the banks of the Euphrates River. Ninigiku-Ea, the god of waters, gave Utanapishtim a revealing dream. Ea's vision said:

> Reed House! reed house! Wall! wall!
> Hear, O reed house! Understand, O wall!
> O man of Shuruppak, son of Ubartutu:
> Tear down the house and build a boat!
> Abandon wealth and seek living things!
> Spurn possessions and keep alive living beings!
> Make all living things go up into the boat . . .[1]

The sage obeyed the message, left his belongings, tore down his house, and, with its materials, built a ship. Following the command, he brought pitch, oil, and wine aboard, sacrificed oxen, and beheaded sheep. On the seventh day, the boat was launched with difficulty. All of Utanapishtim's family as well as the artisans who built the boat went aboard. Field animals and wild beasts were taken to the ship's six decks. When a storm threatened, Puzur-Amurri, the boatman, closed the last hatchways and took command.

1 *The Epic of Gilgamesh*, p. 97.

At dawn the sky filled with black clouds, and torrents of rain came down. Enlil, the brave counselor of the Father of the Gods, let loose the deluge and hurled destruction at humankind. The tempest submerged the mountains. For six days and six nights the wind blew and the storm from the south swept over the earth. The storm did not stop until the seventh day, the day when Utanapishtim's ship came to rest on Mount Nisir.

Men and beasts left the ship, and on the summit of the mountain, seven fires were lit with reeds, cedar, myrtle, and incense. Enlil, now pacified, took the hands of Utanapishtim and his wife and made them kneel before him. He touched their foreheads and blessed them, saying:

> Previously Utanapishtim was a human being.
> But now let Utanapishtim and his wife become like us, the gods!
> Let Utanapishtim reside far away, at the Mouth of the Rivers.

The epic of Gilgamesh, a poem that included the Utanapishtim story, was preserved in the clay tablets upon which the Akkadians and Assyrians wrote their literatures. The Gilgamesh story, however, had already been written with sharpened reeds on fresh clay many centuries before by skilled Sumerian scribes. According to the specialists, the epic must have been finished in the Sumerian language in about the twenty-fifth century

The city of Shuruppak, Utanapishtim's home, was founded around the twenty-eighth century   There is some question whether the deluge and Utanapishtim's deeds were already known in the swampy lands flooded by the Euphrates even before he was given that name and before the Sumerians perfected their cuneiform writing. It is difficult to certify the birth of a myth. Its components emerge, like the great rivers, from the confluence of innumerable and distant currents.

After their consolidation, myths take on more definite forms, particularly when, at culminating points of their existence, they are crystallized into written texts. Two of the narratives about the flood are joined in the Bible to tell us about the patriarch who, like a new Adam, gave origin to all of humanity. Because of this dual source, we find some small discrepancies in the text of the Bible. One concerns the animals Noah took into the ark. Like his predecessor, Utanapishtim, Noah took pairs of the beasts that were to be saved from the flood aboard his ship. According to the Yahwist source, Noah took into the ark seven pairs of each of the species of pure animals: "Of every clean animal, take with you seven pairs, a male and its mate" (Gen. 7:2).[2] The other version, called the priestly source, says that the patriarch took with him only one male and one female of each species: "Of all other living creatures you should bring two into the ark, one male and one female, that you may keep them alive with you" (Gen. 6:19). Despite these small differences, the final version is so forceful that it has moved people throughout the centuries.

Of course the Sumerian and the Biblical versions have important differences. Some are fundamental, such as the reason for the flood. In the Sumerian myth, it was decided upon by the assembled gods. In the Bible, the destruction of nearly all life on the face of the earth was because of Yahweh's heartfelt anger and sorrow about having created human beings.

Other differences between the two versions are merely in the details. The boats, for example, which, according to both versions, were built in seven days, do not correspond to each other in either shape or dimensions. Utanapishtim's ship (ten dozen cubits high on each side and ten dozen cubits on each side of its square deck)—basically a cube that sank two-thirds of its volume into the water—contrasts with Noah's elongated ark (three hundred cubits long, fifty cubits wide, thirty cubits high).

The messages given by birds in the two stories are also different. After his boat stopped, Utanapishtim sent out a dove, which

2 Biblical texts are taken from *The New American Bible*.

came back because it could not find a place to land. Next he released a swallow, which, on its return, announced that the waters were still high. At last he sent out a crow, which did not return, signaling that the waters had subsided. Noah's ark came to rest on the Ararat mountains. The patriarch released a crow, which kept going out and returning until the waters diminished. Afterward, he released a dove, which found no place to perch. After seven days, Noah again sent out the dove, and it returned with an olive branch in its beak to announce that the waters had gone down. After another seven days, the dove flew away and did not return (Gen. 8:6–12).

Another important version of the flood is the one given in the Koran. Muslim scholars believe that in Noah's story there are prophetic allusions to Mohammed's opponents in Mecca. This was not a universal deluge but rather Allah's punishment of the unbelievers. Noah was sent by Allah to preach the true faith, but the chieftains who wished to continue worshipping the gods Wad, Sowa, Yaghuth, Ya'uq, and Nasr did not accept the words of the messenger (Koran 71:23).[3] They said:

> This man is but a mortal like you, feigning himself your superior. Had Allah willed it, He could have sent down angels. Nor did such a thing happen to our forefathers. He is surely possessed. Keep an eye on him awhile. (Koran 23:23–25)

Noah complained to Allah about the people who called him a liar. Then he was given the revelation. He built the ark, went aboard with his family and the believers, and brought a pair of every animal species aboard the ship. Divine punishment came forth as gouts of water that gushed forth in the valley. Waves rose like mountains, and the unbelievers perished.

The myth about the flood came to America with the Euro-

---

3 Koranic texts are from *The Koran*.

pean invasion. In Mesoamerica, there were already myths about a universal flood, at the end of which the gods erected the four posts that separated the sky from the earth. They began the march of time by combining the forces of terrestrial cold and celestial heat. Mayas told Bishop Landa that after the flood's destruction, the *bacaboob,* the four brothers who held up the sky, survived.[4] The *Chilam Balam of Chumayel* says that after the heavens collapsed and the earth sank, after the waters (which had erupted in a single burst) subsided, the four *bacaboob* gods took their places to create order again.[5]

Among the Nahua of the high Central Plateau of Mexico, the deluge myth deals with the union of the two opposing forces that, as they circulate through the four posts, create time. Both forces are represented symbolically in the myth: the warm, dry, celestial, vital force by fire, and the cold, wet, subterranean, death force by the dead fish that remained on the earth after the flood. Tata and Nene, the couple who built a boat and traveled in it during the deluge, committed a great sin when they combined the two forces as they roasted the dead fish and sent smoke to the sky. They were punished for their effrontery: the gods beheaded them and changed them into dogs.[6] Thanks to their error, however, the orderly movement of the world began.

On the basis of these and similar myths, the indigenous Mexican tradition continues to produce interesting narrations. Today, in that immense territory, one hears, in various Mesoamerican languages, tales like that of a farmer who cut down a grove and the next day found that it had grown back again. When he investigated the reason for the miracle, a deity told him that waters would flood the land and he should build a boat to save himself. The farmer built the vessel, climbed aboard, and kept sailing un-

4 Landa, *Relación de las cosas de Yucatán,* p. 62.
5 *The Book of Chilam Balam of Chumayel,* p. 100.
6 *Leyenda de los soles,* p. 120.

til the waters receded. Some versions of the myth say that a female dog, which afterward changed into a woman, accompanied
him, or that when he disembarked, he roasted and ate the remains of fish that had died when the floodwaters disappeared.

There are also many versions of the Mesoamerican flood
myth that include teachings of the missionaries. As was to be expected, the biblical tradition influenced indigenous narratives in
different ways and to varying degrees. There are versions in
which foreign elements and personages invade the tale, even
though at the end of the myth the hero joins a cold substance
(earth brought from hell by a crow) with a hot substance (fire
brought from hell by a fox). Or the vessel used is not the hol-
lowed trunk of an amate tree (fig, *Ficus* sp.) but a box, the literal
translation of "ark." The biblical dove may be added to the fox
and the crow. The protagonist sends the dove to see whether the
earth is dry. The dove sinks its claws into the mud, soaked with
the blood of those who died in the flood, and ever since that
time the bird has had red feet. Finally, the protagonist, like Noah
in the Bible, prepares an intoxicating drink—in this case,
mescal—and when he is drunk, he shows his naked parts. His
sons, like Shem, Ham, and Ja'pheth, produce the different races.[7]

The previous tale is told by the Mixe of Oaxaca. In Yucatán,
the biblical myth about the drunken, naked Noah, insulted by his
sons, also explains the creation of the races. The Maya who tell
the story do not mention the flood, but in their version the three
sons of the drunken hero produce the Negroes, the Indians, and
the white people. The first two sons insulted their father and were
marked by the darkness of their skin, but the third son's skin was
white because he was innocent. The first two were condemned
to hard labor to support themselves, while the third was destined
to do only light work.[8] The myth is outrageously colonial.

7 Miller, *Cuentos mixes,* pp. 100–104.
8 Redfield, *The Folk Literature of a Yucatecan Town,* pp. 8–10.

What a wonderful history of myths! It extends back for mil-
lennia because mythology is one of the great creations of humankind. Myth, oral by nature, was present when the different
cultures perfected the first writing systems, and myths formed
the core of the sacred books. Alive and active, the divine adventures reflect the deepest preoccupations of human beings, their
most intimate secrets, their glories and their shames.

Today, we consider mythology to be one of the great achievements of humanity, but one that is obsolete. We recognize the
literary beauty of myths, their influence on the most diverse
artistic fields, their hermeneutical potential in the study of distant societies, their psychological depth, and the role they played
in the ideological processes of the past. Yet nowadays we consider them to be anachronistic. We forget, in the false universal-
ization of our scientific vision, that myth still performs its
functions in the lives of a great many of the world's inhabitants.

Remember the deeds of the ancient Noah. Three great religions are ruled by the texts that tell his story. Jews, Christians,
and Muslims narrate the episodes of the deluge in their sacred
books. For some of them, the fundamentalists of any of the
three religions, the patriarch's adventures actually happened.
Other believers find a veiled prophetic revelation in them. Others appreciate them as allegory, and still others recognize in the
story a beautiful expression of their religious tradition. How
many among them accept the supernatural character of the text?
No doubt millions. As for the rest, and even for nonbelievers,
the adventure of the ancient Noah will always be one of the
founding elements of culture. Let us not, then, regard mythology as an anachronistic remnant of our history. Let us see it as
alive and functioning.

Indeed, mythology can be a topic of great general interest.
The strongholds of the specialists, whether science, philosophy,
theological exegesis, literature, or art, are too narrow. Studies of
mythology should be widely disseminated.

Convinced of this, in 1990 I decided to write some essays about myths of the Mesoamerican religious tradition. One of my intentions was to write for the general public in the same way I write for my colleagues: through a series of proposals, arguments, expressed doubts, and suggestions that reflect the daily reality of scientific study. I rejected a magisterial exposition based upon supposedly unchangeable truths. I wanted to involve readers in the problems, call their attention to some plausible suppositions, and give data for their evaluation.

That kind of project presupposed a particular kind of reader. I imagined one who would not have the knowledge of a historian or an anthropologist specializing in religion, but I also wanted to maintain a normal dialogue with my colleagues, making these essays a continuation of discussions published in scholarly works or presented in academic forums. I wanted to write for lay persons without excluding scholars. That limited the size of my audience. I needed readers who were interested in religious topics, knowledgeable to some extent about history and the indigenous traditions of Mexico and Central America, and open to reading critically.

Finding such readers was not a simple task. The obvious solution was to select an appropriate magazine in which to publish the essays. It seemed to me that the best one would be *México Indígena,* and my choice was a complete success. Beginning in September 1990, in each successive number, the articles were published under the generic name "Mythologies," and after the magazine, for reasons amply explained by its editors, changed its name to *Ojarasca,* the series continued until April 1992.[9]

I did not publish many articles in *Ojarasca*. A heavy work load made me suspend the project, and I had to stop an activity I had grown to like very much. Now, once again, I wish to thank *Méx-*

---

9 The name *Ojarasca* is a play on words referring to the eyes (*ojos*) of the readers rather than to fallen leaves (*hojarascas*).

ico Indígena and *Ojarasca* and, in particular, Hermann Bellinghausen, its director, Ramón Vera, its editor, and Blanca Sedeño, who was in charge of public relations, for their cooperation.

This volume includes eighteen articles published in *México Indígena* and *Ojarasca*. Minor changes have been made to the original versions. A full bibliography is added at the end of the book.

Mexico, D.F., rainy season, 1992.

The Rabbit
on the Face of
the Moon

Before me I have the reproduction of a beautiful Buddhist image. The original is in the Yota Temple in the district of Kagawa on the island of Shikoku. It is part of a series of twelve illustrations portraying the Guardian gods. This one is Gatten (Moon-Sky). The work is a wood engraving on paper, and the colophon gives the name of the engraver and printer, Sou-un, as well as the date of publication, the twenty-first day of the third month of 1407. The deity has the lunar disk in its hands, and a crouching hare can be seen in the disk.

The image reminds me of the great cultural diversity there is in the perception of reality. Although the moon always shows us the same face, the different cultures of the world have seen very different shapes on it—sometimes a crouching hare, sometimes an old woman carrying a bundle of wood on her back, sometimes the image of a chubby round face. Nevertheless, despite the multiplicity of images, there are notable similarities. Different groups of people, in spite of the great distances separating them, have perceived some parts of nature in almost the same way. Why? Often it is just a coincidence. The way reality is perceived is due to a combination of the inner nature of humans with external reality. A rabbit is seen on the face of the moon? Let us say that the craters on the moon produce shadows that can make people believe they are seeing a familiar shape, and by

Figure 1. Three representations of the moon as a vessel containing a rabbit inside (*Codex Borgia,* pl. 10, 55, 71).

some coincidence, in some traditions it is seen as a small, crouching mammal.

I was reminded of this because just as the Yota Temple image depicted a crouching rabbit on the moon, so the Mesoamerican tradition also said there was a rabbit on the face of the moon. Several Mesoamerican pictographs and sculptures show the moon as a vessel containing the small mammal (figs. 1 and 2).

Myths explain the presence of the rabbit on the moon's face. In a Mexica myth recorded by Friar Bernardino de Sahagún in the sixteenth century, the gods gathered in Teotihuacan and asked one another who would be responsible for lighting up the world.[1] Tecuciztecatl (Dweller of the Place of the Marine Snail), a rich god, offered to illuminate the earth's surface, but the gods wanted another candidate to accompany him. No one had the courage to do so, and every nominee excused himself. Finally, the gods turned to Nanahuatzin (Pimply One), a poor, sickly god, and said to him, "Let it be you who gives the light, Pimply One," and the sick god accepted.

Both of the chosen gods spent four days of penance on the enormous pyramids of the Sun and the Moon. As offerings, Tecuciztecatl brought precious quetzal feathers and balls of gold

1 Sahagún, *Historia general de las cosas de Nueva España,* vol. 2, book 7, chapter 2, pp. 479–82.

Figure 2. A Mixtec representation of the moon on the Tlaxiaco stela.

thread in which to imbed the thorns for self-mutilation. Some of the thorns were made of precious stones rather than agave. The ones that were to be covered with blood were of red coral. Tecuciztecatl burned the finest aromatic resin. In contrast, Nanahuatzin, the sick god, brought as offerings three handfuls of green reeds and balls of grass to hold the thorns, which were sharp agave tips with which he had pierced his body and which he had anointed with his own blood. Instead of aromatic resin, Nanahuatzin burned the scabs from his own pustules.

Once the penance was over, the two gods got ready for the sacrifice. Tecuciztecatl was dressed in a headdress called "jar of white feathers" and a small cloth vest. Nanahuatzin, in contrast, was dressed in paper. As the time for sacrifice drew near, a bonfire was kindled for the cremation of the two gods. The fire was kept burning for four days, and on the last night the gods lined up in two rows while the two who were to be sacrificed placed themselves in front of the fire. The gods asked Tecuciztecatl to throw himself in first. As a wealthy god, that honor belonged to him. Tecuciztecatl tried to throw himself into the fire but drew back when he felt the heat of the flames. Four times he tried, failed, and retreated. Then, since a fifth attempt was not permitted, the gods turned to the sick god and said, "Well, Nanahuatzin, you try." The sick god closed his eyes and cast himself into the flames on the first attempt, causing the fire to crackle. The rich god, ashamed of his cowardice, followed his companion. Both of them were consumed by the flames.

After their cremation, the other gods sat down to wait for the sun's appearance. Dawn made all of the sky red, but the gods did not know from which direction the sun would emerge. Some gods, among them the wind god, Quetzalcoatl, correctly said that the sun would rise in the east. At last, Nanahuatzin came forth in all his brilliance, converted into the sun. Afterward, Tecuciztecatl emerged as the moon, also in the east and with the same intense light.

That bothered the gods. It was not right for the sky to have two astral bodies that shone with the same intensity. They agreed that the moon's light should be diminished, and one of the gods ran to strike Tecuciztecatl's face with a rabbit. Ever since that time, the moon's light has been fainter than the sun's, and the moon's face has retained the dark image of being struck by the rabbit's body.

This myth is probably quite ancient, much older than the sixteenth century when people told it to Sahagún. Perhaps it had been transmitted over the centuries by other Mesoamerican groups, before the Mexica arrived in the lake region of the high Central Plateau of Mexico. That is very likely, because many myths were held in common by the Maya, Zapotec, Mixtec, Mexica, Huastec, Tarasca, and other Mesoamerican peoples from the earliest times.

But was it the myth that caused Mesoamerican people to see a rabbit on the moon? It is not likely. Even though myths keep their fundamental elements throughout the centuries without much variation, there are forms of perception that last longer than myths themselves. In the case of the rabbit on the moon, for example, something more basic was involved than people's simple perception of a figure when they looked into the night sky. A whole complex of beliefs and practices included the idea that a small mammal, or its image, was on the moon. That complex of beliefs and practices was linked to the daily productive life of the people, to their ritual acts, to their ideas about the body's functions, and so forth.

The rabbit was on the moon, but the rabbit was an animal also associated with pulque, a drink made of fermented agave sap, with the south, and with the cold nature of things. The moon was the celestial body related to intoxication, to the changes involved in fermentation, to menstruation, and to pregnancy. There were many other links between the rabbit and the moon in ancient Mesoamerican concepts, and many of those ideas continue to exist among indigenous Mexican peoples today.

The concepts seem to have more solidity and permanence than the myths do themselves. What kind of evidence supports this proposal? The evidence is that after the Spanish conquest, concepts linking the rabbit and the moon to each other and both of them to fermentation and natural cycles remained, whereas the myth about Nanahuatzin and Tecuciztecatl, as told by the Mexica, disappeared. Other myths about the rabbit and the moon, however, have not disappeared. They continue to be told by Mexican natives, and today they are numerous and diverse. Two of them follow.

Among the Chinantec, who live in the state of Oaxaca, it is said that the sun and the moon were two children, brother and sister. The small sun and moon killed an eagle with shiny eyes. The moon took the right eye, which was made of gold, and the sun took the left eye, which was made of silver. After a long walk, the moon felt thirsty. The sun promised to tell her where to find water if she would trade him the eagle's eye, but he told his sister not to drink the water until the Rabbit Priest had blessed the well. The moon disobeyed him, and her brother struck her in the face with the Rabbit Priest. That is why the moon has that mark on her face.[2]

The other myth is told by Tzotzil people of Pinola in the state of Chiapas. The incident occurred at a town fair. A woman and her son had come to amuse themselves on the mechanical rides. They got on the Ferris wheel. The mother carried a rabbit with her. Many envious men at the fair were angry because the child and his mother had been able to get on the wheel in their first try, and they threw rocks at them. One of the rocks hit the woman in the eye. The wheel gyrated, lifting the child and his mother up into the sky. The child was converted into the sun

2 This story was told by Marcelino Mendoza in 1942. See Weitlaner and Castro, *Usila (morada de colibríes)*, pp. 197–202, and Carrasco and Weitlaner, "El Sol y la Luna."

and the mother into the moon, but she did not shine as brightly as the sun because she had been struck in the eye.[3]

From these two stories, it is easy to see that the mythical adventures are secondary in importance to the more profound mythical concepts. The concepts to which the adventures refer are, for example, the cause of the initial difference in brilliance between the sun and the moon, the origin of the shift in who was to have more power initially (the mother over the child, the owner of the gold eye over the owner of the silver eye, the rich, healthy god over the poor, sickly one) and at the end (the sun over the moon), and the existence of the rabbit's image on the face of the moon.[4]

A particular perception, then, does not derive simply from the adventure told in a myth. To the contrary, several myths refer, a posteriori, to that particular perception, which was once tied strongly to concepts and practices rooted in the daily lives of the people.[5]

3 Hermitte, *Poder sobrenatural y control social,* pp. 24–25.

4 See what Gossen (*Los chamulas en el mundo del sol,* pp. 60, 63–64) says about this inversion of power.

5 See chapter 10, "The Eclipse."

{2}
Myths
and Names

More than a hundred years ago, in 1890, a work was published that transformed studies of religious thought and powerfully influenced anthropology into the beginning of the twentieth century. It was *The Golden Bough*. Even today the book remains one of the most ambitious treatises ever written on the subject of religions—a real encyclopedia, in which Sir James Frazer, with great erudition, takes his readers page by page through an astonishing comparison of the beliefs of peoples who lived widely separated in space, tradition, and social complexity.

Since Frazer's time, theories about religion have developed and changed considerably. Today it is not easy to accept the kinds of comparisons he made, comparisons that failed to consider the historical contexts of the societies that had conceived the religious thought. Yet while it is true that to a great extent religious studies have diverged from Frazer's universalist view, it is also true that *The Golden Bough* continues to be an obligatory text and an important source of information for anyone who studies the beliefs of human societies.

In one chapter of *The Golden Bough*, Frazer examined beliefs about the relationship established between objects and their names. This relationship could be so strong that many groups thought it possible to exert magical power over a person or a thing through its name. A result of this belief, according to Frazer, was the widespread custom of hiding a person's "true" name and substituting for it one that was less dangerous and more socially acceptable. Among societies that had practices based on this belief, Frazer cited the Australians, the ancient Egyptians, the Brahmans, and the Araucanians.[1]

Frazer did not include Mesoamerican groups in his list, but in Mesoamerica, too, some people who believed that damage could be done through a name practiced the custom of hiding from society the name considered to be the most vulnerable. In ancient times the Nahua used several names. One was the calendrical name, the name of the day on which a child received its ritual bath. The name was bestowed while the child was washed with water that had been exposed to the sun that same day. A different name was used openly in society, and still another was a nickname, often referring to some episode in the person's life. The calendrical name might be Yei-Mazatl (3-Deer), while the "official" name might be Ixtlilxochitl (Vanilla Face). The nickname given to a ruler of Mexico-Tenochtitlan was Ilhuicamina (Archer of the Sky).

The most important name was the first, the calendrical name. It was the name not only of the person but also of his or her *tonalli,* or soul-destiny. It is probably more accurate to say that the name was identified with the soul-destiny. The *tonalli* had to be implanted in the Nahua child by means of the ritual bath. Destinies were the divine forces that the sun emitted each day. One of these forces, corresponding to the day of the ceremony, was put into the child through the rite, and it became part of his or her animistic being. Parents could choose the best destiny available for their child from the cycle of thirteen days in which the child was born, but they could not delay the rite until the following set of thirteen because the child did not belong to that

1 Frazer, *The New Golden Bough,* pp. 235–39.

cycle. The soul was vulnerable through the name. Because it was linked to destiny and the soul, the birth name had to be kept secret so that no one could put the person under a spell by pronouncing it in an incantation.

The destiny name was not, however, kept secret among all of the Mesoamerican groups. In the Mixtec codices, calendrical name glyphs were often shown next to the images of rulers and their wives. The same thing occurred in documents written in Latin script during colonial times. In them, Mixtec personages were usually denoted by their destiny names.

If names were considered to be objects independent of the beings they designated but at the same time closely linked to them by supernatural ties, it is logical that they would also be found in creation myths. Indeed, names appeared as things to be created in Mesoamerican myths, and they continue to appear in the indigenous myths of Mexico and Central America. This is true not only of proper names, such as those of the gods, but also of the common names of animals, plants, and things. It should be noted that in ancient times the gods, like human beings, had names that referred to some of their attributes, as well as calendrical names. For example, the fire god could be called Huehue-teotl (Ancient God) and also Nahui-Acatl (4-Reed).

In August 1972, in the Sierra of Jalisco, I heard a Huichol myth about the birth of the sun. The narrator, Jesús Rentería, told how the primordial animals marveled at the first dawn and asked each other what would be the name of the one who would daily light up the sky. None of the animals mentioned the name of the astral body until the turkey dared to do so, saying, "It is going to be called the sun." In a violent reaction to the turkey's interference, the other animals tore the skin off a serpent and hung it around the turkey's neck. Ever since then, the turkey has had its fleshy protuberances. The quail and the rabbit also uttered the name of the sun but, fearing punishment, ran away as they said it. The other animals tried to capture them among the reeds. They were able to grab them only by their tails, which they yanked off. Since then, the rabbit and the quail have been tailless.

This myth reminds me of another from the state of Oaxaca, told by the Mixe. In this myth, Christ appears with two European animals, the rooster and the donkey. It should be mentioned that in the myths and beliefs of contemporary Mexican and Central American natives, the figure of the sun is often replaced by Christ's. The Mixe say that when Christ was born, only the rooster was awake, and the bird announced with a loud cry, "Jesus Christ is born-n-n!" The donkey, to the contrary, was still asleep and could only utter the complaint, "Ou-ou-ou-ou!" Ever since then, as punishment for his laziness, that cry has been the donkey's characteristic sound. He was the animal who failed to name Christ.[2]

According to a Nahua tale from the Sierra of Puebla, it was not Jesus' name that originated the expression of fear or admiration—"Jesus!"—but the reverse. The opossum, the famous marsupial that is often a personage in Mexican stories and myths, went to steal fire in order to warm the Virgin's newborn child. Upon arriving at the doorway of the birthplace, the opossum realized that its tail had caught fire while it was carrying the flame away. Frightened and in pain, it cried out, "Oh, Jesus! Oh, Jesus!" and from this expression the child was named Jesus.[3]

In a Nahua myth from the state of Durango, the insulting epithet "mule" was the origin of the animal's name, and not the reverse. Native people told the famous investigator Konrad T. Preuss that one day the goddess Tonantzi was riding along a river bank. A young man who was sunning himself on the sand got up suddenly as the goddess went by. Frightened by the youth's action, the animal that was carrying Tonantzi threw the goddess

2 Miller, *Cuentos mixes,* p. 207.
3 Taggart, *Nahuat Myth and Social Structure,* pp. 103–104.

off. The furious goddess stood up. She told the boy, "You will be called alligator." Then she said to her mount, "You will be called mule, and you will be sterile." And so the youth who had been resting, lying on the sand under the sun's rays, was the origin of alligators, animals that terrorize travelers on riverbanks with their sudden attacks, while the beast that carried Tonantzi was changed into a sterile mule.[4]

In these origin myths, names and the beings they designate are created in the same primordial adventure. Their nature, however, is different, so the main myth takes time to explain the source of the name. Thus two beings are created, the one named and the name itself.

---

4 Preuss, *Mitos y cuentos nahuas de la Sierra Madre Occidental,* p. 173.

{3}

Invention and Discovery in the Mythical Concept of the World

A belief in mythical creation and a belief in evolution are two very different approaches to reality. The notion of origins in myth is radically opposed to the notion of origins in the evolutionary concept of nature and society, because in myth things are created and established in a single stroke. In mythical accounts, created beings possess, from the time of their first appearance, the characteristics that will be essential to them. This is clearly shown in the many complex accounts in which the gods establish most of the world, beginning with a chaotic mass of obscure, humid, and amorphous primordial existence. The myth ends when each of the classes of beings is completely formed. Through myth, the existing classes acquire the last of their attributes. The final acts of the divine adventures result in the totality of the creatures.

Origin stories follow the same pattern. They are simple narratives with a festive flavor found at the margins between true myths and stories produced for the mere pleasure of fictional invention. They are tales in which animals, plants, minerals, and human beings themselves begin to exist with the last touch of a deity, the last episode of an adventure, the last consequence of a transgression, or, to sum it up, the last cause that produces the totality of the finished work.

Stories of this kind abound in all the traditions. Today the

Lenca, a Honduran ethnic group whose ancestors were neighbors of the Mesoamericans, end their tale about the deer with its stealing the two bumps on the head of the frog and converting them into the majestic adornment of its own head.[1] The deer's shape was almost complete; that decoration was the last feature the species needed. The Lenca tale ends the creative process not only by completing the deer's body with the antlers but also by explaining why the antlers do not last throughout the year. The theft becomes one of the elements of the account. Antlers were alien to the already formed, almost complete deer. Because of this lack of true ownership, the late acquisition has to be repeated each year when the new growth on the antlers appears.

The mythical concept unites the organizing principles of the world by running what is cultural and what is natural according to the same cosmic laws. This is done by combining conceptions that uniformly regularize the processes of everything that exists. The primordial creation of natural beings becomes the primordial creation of cultural entities, resulting in a strongly conservative vision. From this point of view, humans do not change historically because of technical and social transformations. Instead, they have, through cosmic, divine order, a permanent, immutable condition. Everything that is cultural is a part of creation: institutions, social differences, knowledge, techniques—all are conceived of as being born in a primordial dawn that established existing society in all its complexity.

There are myths that explicitly account for some aspects of the creation of cultural artifacts in primordial time. An example is a myth of the ancient Colima Indians. In the sixteenth century, Juan Suárez de Cepeda wrote that the Colima Indians, inhabitants of a territory that at the time belonged to New Granada, believed in a primordial flood of the world. As the surface of the earth dried, the vapors created not only the different

---

1 Carias et al., *Tradición oral indígena de Yamaranguila*, pp. 115–16.

animals but also large earthen vats, tools, and human weapons.[2] For the people of Colima, these cultural artifacts were not the products of human action but something that emerged from the great common birth of what is natural and what is cultural.

In the mythical concept of the world, society occupies a secondary place to the supernatural. It is not the source of the principal inventions and discoveries but the recipient of divine gifts. That was the way the ancient inhabitants of the high Central Plateau of Mexico thought. Their beliefs emphasized the concept of donations from their gods.

The *calpulli* was an important basic unit for the Nahua, whose social structure was based on the articulation of the economic activities of specialized groups. Each *calpulli* was formed of families linked by common residence, joint ownership of land, strong cooperative obligations, strong administrative unity with respect to the central government, autonomy in regard to the intimate life of the group, and, above everything else, a common occupation. The ancient Nahua attributed the origins of their occupations to the gifts each of the ancestors had given to their descendants. Members of the group believed in a common ancestor who was fused with the *calpulteotl,* the patron god of the group. That personage had given them the knowledge and instruments of their particular occupation. He was the remote inventor of the occupation and its tools.

In the city of Mexico-Tenochtitlan, the Mexica capital, for example, the district called Tlamatzinco was protected by the god Izquitecatl, to whom was attributed the discovery of the process of fermenting pulque. Men in the Tlamatzinco *calpulli* were the ones who made pulque. Just as Izquitecatl gave his *calpulli* its craft, so, too, the goddess Tzapotlatenan taught her *calpulli* how to make *uxitl,* a medicinal ointment highly esteemed in ancient times. And so Yacatecuhtli (patron of the merchants) invented

2 Suárez de Cepeda, *Relación de los indios colimas de la Nueva Granada,* p. 18.

commerce, Xipe Totec, metallurgy, Cipactonal, weaving and divination, Nappatecuhtli, the making of mats, Cinteotl, the carving of precious stones, Opochtli, the oars, ropes, nets, and darts used to hunt waterfowl, Coyotl Inahual, feather mosaics, Huixtocihuatl, the making of salt, Coatlicue, flower arrangement, and Camaxtli, the techniques and tools for hunting.

There were occasions, however, when an invention or a discovery could not be attributed to the initial time because it was too recent or was very specialized in its use. Such cases were explained by miracles. Divine participation was not eliminated this way; a miracle still attributed the origin of everything important to the gods.

One of the paths a miracle could follow was that of revelation during a dream or during a transitory death. An example of this kind of miracle can be found in the work of Hernando Ruiz de Alarcón, who in the seventeenth century recorded the account of an elderly native doctor called Domingo Hernández. According to Ruiz de Alarcón, the old doctor assured him that he had died and then returned to life. He said that in the other world he had obtained his healing technique, which had been given to him by supernatural personages. Those personages had then ordered him to return to life in order to benefit his fellow beings with his therapeutic knowledge.[3]

The gods, therefore, were considered to be the creators of all the important techniques, either in primordial time or through miraculous interventions. But there is no rule without its exception, and in the historical sources can be found an example of a discovery attributed not to the gods but to chance. It appears in *Recordación florida,* a seventeenth-century history by Francisco Antonio Fuentes y Guzmán that comes from Guazacapán, a town on the southern coast of Guatemala. The tale refers to the effects of a small, poisonous fruit called *canjura* that people mixed

3 Ruiz de Alarcón, *Tratado de las idolatrías . . . de las razas aborígenes,* pp. 157–60.

with meat and left in the fields to kill coyotes.[4] The plant was not poisonous to all animals but specifically to coyotes and dogs. As the story has it, turkeys could feed on *canjura* without risk because they were immune to its toxin. The poison remained in their bones, however, and if dogs or coyotes ate the remains of a turkey that had fed on the fruit, they would be poisoned.

The story also tells about the discovery of the effects of *canjura* on human beings. A particularly beautiful Indian woman was married to an Indian chief who suffered from a skin disease known as *jiote* (impetigo). Dissatisfied with her marriage and disgusted by her husband's disease, the woman decided to become a widow by poisoning the sick man. She slipped *canjura* into a cup of chocolate and waited for it to take effect. The chief, after drinking the chocolate, felt intense heat and almost deadly pains that lasted for twenty hours. Afterward, he perspired profusely, and in doing so produced an unexpected result. The sweat cleared the scabs that had covered his skin until he was again completely healthy. The chief, instead of dying from the poison, had a crisis that completely cured him.

The story ends too conventionally. The beautiful woman repented, reconciled with her husband, and loved him again. They lived together happily until the chief's death. Then the once frustrated and repentant killer, now a widow, confessed her sin and revealed the marvelous virtues of *canjura*.[5]

And with that story, the discovery was removed from the realm of the divine and placed at least in the realm of chance.

4 Translator's note: *Canjura* is perhaps *Thevetia peruviana*.
5 Fuentes y Guzmán, *Recordación florida*, vol. 2, p. 117.

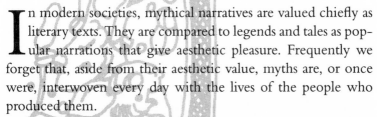

{4}
Clay

In modern societies, mythical narratives are valued chiefly as literary texts. They are compared to legends and tales as popular narrations that give aesthetic pleasure. Frequently we forget that, aside from their aesthetic value, myths are, or once were, interwoven every day with the lives of the people who produced them.

People forged myths from their daily experiences. Their mythical personages were the invisible beings they believed were all around—in the cultivated fields, in the jungle or the desert, in the ocean, in the immensity of the nocturnal sky, or in the corners of their own houses. They put into narratives the beings they imagined to be their permanent and imperceptible neighbors. They saw those personages' behavior in the regularity of natural processes, and by that regularity they defined the strong characteristics of the heroes of the mythical adventures.

But not everything was regular. Daily events had their contingencies, and so a capriciousness was added to the character of the personages. Mythical beings had will power that humanized their behavior. Because of it, they were so similar to human beings that they could have their own histories, carry out adventures, and act on their passions.

Therefore, the great distance that we suppose between the surroundings in which the believer acts and the celestial or infernal world of the gods' adventures does not, in fact, exist. At any rate, those heavens and hells are only the dwellings of human beings transformed by an imagination nourished by daily life. Myth was born from the soil. The mother goddess was fertile and terrible because the farmer's land either produced or denied the harvest. The lord of the forest was jealous of his dominions because the hunter himself felt strange when he entered the forest.

If daily life was the medium in which myth developed, then reciprocally, myth became a tool and a guide for daily life. As a guide it reinforced their knowledge of nature and material things and of the succession of temporal cycles. It also reinforced their daily activities as well as their behavior toward fellow beings and their obligations to the gods. Myth does not explicitly describe or prescribe. It does not show clearly the laws of the cosmos. It is a form of synthetic expression of the occupations and preoccupations of humans in daily contact with their neighbors and with nature. As an instrument, myth teaches, imposes or supports reasons, and justifies behaviors. In short, it is much more than a narrative. It is an institution of enormous utility that combines beliefs with practical knowledge.

People who live in modern societies find it difficult to conceive of such a combination. Our existence is composed of separate parts that tilt dangerously toward independence. We try to disconnect our arenas of action and of thought and also progressively to create new compartments within the same sphere. Is this good or bad? It doesn't matter. Modern life requires it to be thus. What must be understood is that the societies we call traditional have much greater congruence between behavior and thought than ours does. That congruence is projected, for the most part, in those societies' concepts of united and imperceptible social and natural laws. Any expression of thought is thus converted into a means of understanding the holistic image of the universe. In that sense, myth is one of the privileged expressions, a true synthesis of the cosmovision.

We Mesoamerican historians are fully aware of this, and we know it for practical reasons. Although we can count on rich sources for the study of ancient traditions, they are not as abundant as we might wish. There are serious gaps in our information about particular subjects. It would be helpful, for example, to find more records of the way land was distributed, of work techniques, of family relationships, of the organization of labor, of the composition of basic social groups, of political systems, and so forth. In our present situation we cannot be satisfied with the scanty specific data from written sources. It is necessary to sharpen our wits and seek indirectly, through different means—such as, among others, the philological analysis of the lexicon or the study of literary texts—for information that we cannot obtain directly. To this end, myth as a privileged expression can help us considerably. For instance, we can learn a lot about concepts of nobility from references to a primeval time when Quetzalcoatl, the mythical ancestor of the nobles, obtained for his descendants the exclusive power to govern the people.

A study of myth gives new dimensions to the historical knowledge of social organization, family relationships, and ancient ways of doing things. It allows us to understand complex institutions as they interact in society. It transcends the cold abstractions that seem to lose their human origin in studies in which charts, formulas, graphs, or measurements predominate. No doubt those tables and formulas are indispensable to an understanding of reality, but they are not everything, because institutions do not exist alone and independent in the midst of the complexity of social life.

Myth cannot be studied merely as literary expression. If we search for the central obsession of mythical creation that has predominated in Mesoamerica from ancient times until the present, we see clearly that it was the alternation of the dry seasons and the rainy seasons. In the lives of farmers, the seasonal drama became the cyclical succession of life and death, of the above and the below, of superior and inferior, of feminine and masculine. In short, it solidified into a universal law in which opposing values, rather than occupying the extreme ends of a graduated line, revolved in a circle of alternation of dominance.

There was no Manichean duality in Mesoamerican myths. Mesoamerican gods were neither absolutely good nor absolutely evil. In the myths of indigenous Mesoamericans, as in their morals and their practical daily lives, only the wise relativity of the transitory, of the contingent, existed; what was merely adequate, what was opportune, did not rule. Rains were the expression of death, which produced life. Dry periods were life, but they also represented a consumption that led to death. There was no confrontation between the positive and the negative but an alternation of causes—the cosmic law that every living thing must die and that death is the source of all forms of life.

The bargain a farmer made with the land and with the annual harvest was achieved by a complex group of techniques, but those techniques were, in their turn, part of a lively human dialogue. We can see this among all contemporary indigenous peoples. Eckart Boege, in his book *Los mazatecas ante la nación,* describes important parts of that dialogue, in which a farmer enters into a relationship with the guardians of the earth (the "owners," or *chikones*), to whom he gives offerings in order to get their permission to cultivate the earth. Agricultural work is considered to be a transitory activity based on a loan, on a temporary appropriation of the land, which is naturally savage.

The farmer also begs the *chikones* to tolerate his labor and not to trap his spirit or put serpents into him. The earth is a living being; it is Mother Earth. To cut her or burn her is to offend her, "to wound her." The damage done must be paid for by adequate worship. The field is profoundly humanized. Chumaje, the lady of vegetation, nurses the plants daily so they will grow. A slight hum can be heard as Chumaje suckles them, and a breeze moves the stalks when the goddess rocks and lulls the cornfield. Chumaje is born as a child each morning. She grows through the afternoon and dies at night. Moreover, she grows old as the calendar advances in order to sanction with the force of her age the opportunity for work in the field. After June 20, no one can sow, because by then Chumaje is old and diminished.

Indeed, relationships with the supernatural beings reinforce human techniques for managing agricultural time. The payment the owner of a cornfield makes to Mother Earth as compensation for wounding her is not only a personal deal between believer and goddess but also an order pertaining to the time of harvest and a warning to anyone who wants to steal some maize. The cornfield has been "prayed over." Payment to Mother Earth should be made in the month of Chakjoa (the twenty days from August 9 to 28). No one can touch the ears of maize before the ceremony, and the only one authorized to gather the first grain is the owner of the field himself. The gods will kill anyone else who touches or steals an ear.[1]

Thus among the Mazatec the dates of the religious calendar are the same as those of the agricultural calendar. The Feast of the Dead marks the end of the rainy season. By that time the harvesting of everything sown during the rainy season must be done.

When cultivation techniques and the relationships for appropriating the land are changed, the connections of the people to the supernatural are weakened or disappear. With the loss of traditional forms of life, the peasant also loses the effective life that is a part of his labor. María Ana Portal tells us in *Cuentos y mitos en una zona mazateca* that the indigenous farmer observes the agrarian rituals only in the maize, bean, and chile fields. When he grows sugarcane on land outside the traditional organized space, the Mazatec, as a day laborer, no longer has a relationship with Mother Earth.[2]

---

1 Boege, *Los mazatecos ante la nación*, pp. 148–53.
2 Portal, *Cuentos y mitos en una zona mazateca*, p. 90.

Far from the Mazatec lands, to the south of the Huasteca, the Otomi of San Pablito, too, place little confidence in the foreign crop sugarcane. Jacques Galinier says that sugarcane is called "old man's bone" and that it evokes evil, death, the world of the mestizos. The Lord of Sugarcane is not a beneficent god but a devil.[3] Cane is the antithesis of maize. It should not seem strange, then, that a myth has developed in which the malignant character named Lord of Sugarcane behaves as a troublemaker when Indians approach the place of Christ's birth. The tale is one more synthesis of the complex emotional life of human beings who manage the technique of production. The Lord of Sugarcane embodies all the negative aspects of the alienated land, of the ancient invasion of the black cultivators in the plantations of the Sierra Baja and the coast of Vera Cruz. He also incarnates the evil effects of the alcoholism that comes from the production of liquor made from sugarcane.

---

3 Galinier, *Pueblos de la Sierra Madre,* p. 362.

The Words
of the
Incantation

For a long time before I began to study the magical and re-ligious beliefs of Mesoamerica, I thought that incantations were unrelated words or mere combinations of sounds that had been preserved by an esoteric practice. I believed they were phrases to which the faithful attributed the ability to transform reality. This belief probably resembles the amazement produced in lay believers by the speeches of their magicians and priests. It probably is also similar to the view of many priests and magicians, who, more intent on practical than on speculative matters, simply repeated the words, attributing much of the efficacy of the prayer to its particular wording and little to its possible meaning.

When I studied the ancient Nahua and Maya incantations, I realized the value of the meaning of the discourses. The texts are hard to understand, but it is clear that behind their impenetrability there are codes by which magicians tried to communicate with beings who inhabited a hidden reality.

The Nahua called that intricate form of communicating with invisible forces *nahuallatolli,* which means "secret word," because it derives from *nahualli* (the hidden, the covered) and *tlatolli* (speech, word). The incantations were addressed to the invisible beings. They tried to dissuade those beings from their bad intentions or convince them to help the specialist in handling power. At times the incantation was ferocious: the magician took the risk of threatening the hidden forces to make them comply with his request. He addressed the invisible beings with great familiarity, calling them by their secret names, something that must have made a strong impression on the faithful who heard the words without completely understanding their meaning.

It is interesting that often these secret names referred to the creation of the world. According to Mesoamerican beliefs, the beings of the world were created not in a single, unique moment but by a process ruled by the calendar. Because of this, many of the secret names derive from the calendar. For example, trees were called Ce-Quiahuitl (1-Rain), deer were Chicome-Xochitl (7-Flower), and fire, Nahui-Acatl (4-Reed).

In some cases, names referred directly to the myths of origin. An example is the colonial medical incantation recorded by Hernando Ruiz de Alarcón. The patient's body was called Chicomoztoc, the name of the great mountain in which the various human groups were born.[1] Through this practice the human body and its cavities were equated with the great origin mountain and its seven caves.

Although a myth might be alluded to in an incantation, the content of the myth is not always clear. We must remember that the language of the magician was obscure, and much of it is still incomprehensible to scholars. Additionally, many of the ancient myths were not written down in Latin script. Even though traces of myths appear in religious iconography (pictographic codices or sculptures), no reliable rendition of the words has preserved the ancient narrations for us in just the same way they were told by narrators to their audiences. The full meaning of many of the incantations has not yet been explained, and scholars must use their wits to find the relationships among the various native traditions.

---

1 Ruiz de Alarcón, *Aztec Sorcerers in Seventeenth Century Mexico: The Treatise on Superstitions,* tract 6, chapter 16, p. 182; tract 6, chapter 17, p. 183.

One alternative way to discover the meanings of incantations is to explore accounts of colonial and modern beliefs. Although it may seem strange, even after five centuries of assault on native religions by Christian evangelizers there is still much in current beliefs that can help us understand the beliefs of the Mesoamerican past. This does not mean that during all that time native thought was not profoundly altered. Any religious concept will change a great deal over such a long time, and more so when it is subjected to the aggressive attack of a dominant group. Mesoamerican tradition was so strong, however, that the old way of thinking still influences contemporary thought.

A magical-therapeutic practice from the seventeenth century used the harsh procedure of puncturing a patient's body to expel a personified illness. It was not similar to acupuncture. It was an actual assault on a disease that, according to the beliefs of the time, was conscious, had volition, and could be expelled from the body through a direct attack. In order to harmonize intentions, acts, and words, the native doctor chanted an incantation in which the needle (the thing that pulls the thread, its "intestine") was called *aguilucho* (hawk) and the stomachache was called "serpent."

> Look! White serpent,
> dark serpent, yellow serpent,
> you are damaging the place of the pouch,
> the place of the Spanish broom [*esparto*] box;
> you are harming our flesh rope,
> our intestines of flesh.
> Now the white eagle goes there,
> the dark eagle.
> I did not come for you now;
> I did not come to destroy you.
> Only in a corner, only against the wall,
> I will see that your arm, your venerable foot
> are hidden.

And if you do not obey me,
I will call the venerable eaglet priest;
I will call the brown Chichimec.
He also is dying of thirst;
He also very hungry,
he who drags his intestine . . .[2]

The imagery of this combat was well known. It was the battle related in other, more ancient texts between the falcon called *huactli (Herpetotheres cachinnans cachinnans)* and the serpent, the hawk's usual food. Through it, the success of the therapeutic action was assured; the doctor's procedure paralleled the one occurring in nature.

In order to understand this incantation, it is also necessary to look for symbolic interaction between these two animals in a mythical or ritualistic context. Although this symbolic interaction was not recorded in ancient texts, it exists in our own time for two contemporary native groups, the Huichol and the Mazatec. The former live in Jalisco and Nayarit, and the latter, in Oaxaca. How can we prove that a Nahua symbolic relationship can be found in the beliefs of the Huichol and the Mazatec? Because, in the past, despite great regional variation, there was a common cosmological and religious basis in all of Mesoamerica. Today, for the Huichol, the union of tobacco and its container symbolizes the struggle between hawk and serpent. Tobacco (*yé*) is the falcon, and the bottle gourd, or bule (*kwé*), is the serpent.[3] The fight is symbolically expressed with the word (*yekwé*), that is, the union of the tobacco and the container.[4]

The Mazatec tell a myth about a battle at the time of creation. The serpent, which had no way to defend itself, was taunted by the other beings. Humiliated, it complained to God and re-

2 Ruiz de Alarcón, *Tratado de las idolatrías,* tract 6, chapter 19, p. 159.
3 The bottle gourd is *Lagenaria siceraria.*
4 Furst, "Para encontrar neustra vida: El peyote entre los huicholes," pp. 179–80.

ceived its venom. But the poison was a serious danger to others, and an antidote was needed. The hawk, which kills serpents at sunrise, was created. Today, the patrons of the animals are Catholic saints, revealing an excessive Christian influence.

> At that time [of darkness], the snake was not poisonous. Everyone teased [humiliated] it. Then Saint George and Saint Ignatius, who is the snake's patron saint, complained to the Holy Father, and the Holy Father gave saliva to the snake, so that it would be respected. The saliva became poison. Snakes became dangerous to human beings. The cowboy [a falcon] appeared which killed snakes, calling out as he killed. If it were not for this kind of falcon, there would be all kinds of snakes. And this is the reason snakes come out only at night.[5]

The simple reference to the myth doesn't clarify all the cosmic meaning of the rivalry between the *huactli* and the serpent. But the intent of the seventeenth-century magician-doctors who used the incantation is quite clear. They wanted to connect their actions to a process imbedded in a myth, a cosmic archetype.

5 Boege, *Los mazatecos ante la nación*, p. 102.

{6}
Myths in the Mesoamerican Religious Tradition

Paul Kirchhoff, one of the leading experts on precolonial native societies of Mexico and Central America, established the bases for a systematic and complete study of the peoples who lived in the cultural area we call Mesoamerica. These people were the maize farmers who lived in the southern half of Mexico and in most of Central America. They created the strongly individualized cultures that we now call Olmec, Zapotec, Huastec, Mexica (or Aztec), Tarasca, and by many other names.

All of these people had a common history, and because of it, their technology, their forms of social organization, their beliefs and customs, and indeed all of their cultural baggage comprised a tradition. Obviously, major social transformations took place that made groups differ profoundly from each other, but they were all immersed in the same historical current. Their diverse forms of life and thought made their religious beliefs and practices differ, but in general the bases of their concepts and practices coincided to a remarkable degree.

Many scholars feel that because of the area's historical-cultural unity, it is useful to study the region as a whole, or at least to keep the general Mesoamerican context always in mind when investigating any one of the groups forming the precolonial tradition. In 1943, Paul Kirchhoff coined the term *Mesoamerica* and proposed the defining traits of the *Mesoamerican cultural area*.[1] His proposal focused the archaeological discussion, and since then the term has been widely accepted by scholars.

Mesoamerican anthropology has progressed considerably in the last fifty years. The basic traits Kirchhoff described are no longer valid, according to current knowledge. But the name proposed by the learned German remains, along with scholars' gratitude toward a man who devoted so much of his life to the study of native societies.

Religious unity in Mesoamerica is, of course, a part and a consequence of historical-cultural unity. This unity was noticed long ago. As early as the sixteenth century, when Europeans began to study the native religions, there were people who recognized the relatedness of native beliefs and practices. Friar Bartolomé de las Casas, referring to Indian beliefs in Guatemala, wrote:

> All of this land which is properly called New Spain had, more or less, the same religion and similar gods. It extended to the provinces of Nicaragua and Honduras in one direction, and in the direction of Jalisco, I think it extended to the province of Colima and Culiacán.[2]

In spite of statements like this, scholars disagreed about the degree of unity in Mesoamerican religion. Around the beginning of the twentieth century, a debate began with questions raised by Seler in his study of the mural paintings in Mitla, Oaxaca.[3] A number of scholars participated on both sides of the religious unity question, while others argued for more rigorous comparisons to settle the issue. Among the authors who wrote on this topic were Beyer, Thompson, Caso, Kirchhoff himself,

---

1 Kirchhoff, *Mesoamérica: Sus límites geográficos, composición étnica y carácteres culturales.*

2 Las Casas, *Apologética historia sumaria,* vol. 1, book 3, chapter 124, p. 651.

3 Seler, "Wall Paintings of Mitla."

Jiménez Moreno, Kubler, Hunt, Nicholson, and Rivera Dorado. I include myself in the list, too, because a good part of my book *The Myths of the Opossum* argued that, in spite of great differences in worship, in symbols, and in the particular beliefs found in different regions and at different times, the basic principles of Mesoamerican cosmovision had the same historical development everywhere, and many of the fundamental myths were related to each other.

Many unifying characteristics can be found in Mesoamerican religion. There are similar groups of principal deities and a single basic calendrical mechanism, despite its being expressed at different levels of complexity. Across Mesoamerica we see similarities in rituals, in patterns of priestly organization, in symbolism, in concepts of the cosmos, in types of political organization based on the divine order, and in the magical and religious bases of medicine. And there is identity or similarity among myths. Besides mentioning the coincidences, however, I believe that some characteristics of the tradition that allow us to penetrate deeper into the problem should be emphasized.

First, there is no evidence that the believers themselves differentiated among religions or sects. Second, because the similarity was due to these societies being subjected to the same historical happenings, it is necessary to examine not only the identity or similarity of the religious elements but also the historical process. We must look at both the rapid changes that took place in some aspects of religion and the slow transformation of basic religious principles. Third, religion served as the part of the culture in which the greatest number of interactions took place among the different Mesoamerican peoples, from their alliances to their wars, from commerce to political supremacy or subordination, as if religion were a code that allowed different groups of people to speak a common language for their coexistence.

This situation changed considerably during the colonial period. Native groups, dominated by Europeans and Christianized by force, had less freedom to interact independently and particularly to do so in terms of their own religion. The result was the birth of new forms of religious beliefs and practices. These, as one might suppose, differed considerably from each other, as they still do today. There is a long continuum that approaches the ancient native tradition on one end and Christianity on the other. In general, however, the new forms differ both from the precolonial Mesoamerican religion, because some key elements of the ancient religion have almost completely disappeared, and from the imposed Christianity, because it has not been completely assimilated.

The beliefs and practices issuing from this confluence of Mesoamerican religion and Christianity were not just syncretic mixtures of the two currents. They were adaptive responses to specific social situations. They were colonial religions that arose from the need for a defense against colonial domination. Although they cannot be identified with either of the currents from which they came, they should be recognized as religions registered in both traditions; they belong as much to the Mesoamerican as to the Christian tradition.

Because the new religious systems are part of the Mesoamerican tradition, there are contemporary myths that, in spite of the necessary and normal transformation of stories and beliefs, retain much of the ancient narrations. A notable example is a myth about the origin of maize that appears in a sixteenth-century colonial document in Nahuatl called *Leyenda de los Soles*. It says that after human beings had been created, the gods Apantecuhtli, Huictlolinqui, Tepanquizqui, Tlallamanac, Tzontemoc, and Quetzalcoatl asked each other what the new beings would eat. The red ant had found maize kernels inside Tonacatepetl, the Mountain of Our Sustenance. Quetzalcoatl saw the insect's burden and demanded, "Tell me where you got it." The god had to insist because the insect did not want to reveal its secret. Finally the ant confessed, pointing in the direction of Tonacatepetl.

Knowing the secret, Quetzalcoatl turned himself into a black ant and accompanied the red one to the storage place. Both ants entered the hill. Quetzalcoatl took some kernels of maize from inside and carried them to Tamoanchan, the place where the gods had created humans. There, the gods chewed the food and put the dough on the lips of the recently created humans in order to strengthen them. The result was encouraging, but it was necessary to obtain more seeds in order to continue to nourish humankind. They said, "What will we do with Tonacatepetl?" Quetzalcoatl tied the mountain with ropes and tried to lift it up and carry it, but he couldn't do it.

Two soothsayer gods, Oxomoco and Cipactonal, cast lots with maize kernels in order to find out how to obtain the grain. They concluded that only Nanahuatl could break open the immense coffer. All of the rain gods participated in the project—the blue gods, the white, the yellow, and the red—and in a final effort, Nanahuatl struck the mountain and made it release its treasure. The mountain spilled out white corn, black corn, yellow corn, and red corn. It also released beans, *huauhtli* (amaranth, *Amaranthus* sp.), chia, and *michhuauhtli* (fish amaranth). All the food came under the jurisdiction of the rain gods, the *tlaloque,* who seized the seeds in order to distribute them later to the humans.[4]

Today, four centuries later, very similar versions of that myth can be found in towns in the Maya area. Among them is the one elicited in the 1970s from representatives of the Chol people of Chiapas by Jesús Morales Bermúdez.[5] Just as in the sixteenth-century version, the black ant and the red ant take the grain out of its stone enclosure. Afterward, the rain gods, each identified by his distinctive color, break into the mountain in which the vegetable treasure is kept.

---

4 *Leyenda de los soles,* p. 121.
5 Morales Bermúdez, *On o t'ian: Narrativa indígena chol,* pp. 94–95.

The similarity between the two versions, surprising as much for its endurance over time as for its endurance across geographical distance, can be explained in many ways. It could be that in the Mesoamerican past, a Nahuatl group imposed on the Maya this belief about the origin of corn, or that the Maya were the ones who took the tale to the Nahua on the Central Plateau. Neither of these assumptions, however, is satisfactory. It is more logical to suppose that in the immense territory in which Mesoamerican peoples interacted for century upon century, the myth was produced, as all of the great cultural episodes are produced, by everyone and by no one, through additions, suppressions, and rearrangements, the transformations being confused with the origins. Like so many others, this is a myth that cannot in a strict sense be classified as Maya or Nahuatl or Zapotec or anything else. It is a Mesoamerican myth still alive in the native tradition.

We were watching the movie *The Dreams* of Akira Kurosawa. On the screen a heavy rain was falling on a wall and the entrance to a house, while the sun's rays created sharp, contoured shadows. Martha Rosario, sitting beside me in the theater, said in a low voice, "A doe is giving birth." But in the movie, something else was being said about the luminous rain. A woman was warning Kurosawa as a child that he should not go outside because it was the time when foxes mated, and they did not like to be watched.

I left the movie thinking about Martha Rosario's remark, "A doe is giving birth." It was the usual, almost unconsciously spoken phrase that we employ in our homeland, the northern desert frontier of Mexico, when it rains while the sun is shining. I remembered that I often used to ask myself, as a child, what relationship there was between rain and the birth of a deer. Later, the saying became just one of many that we repeated through habit but whose meaning had disappeared.

I have never heard any saying about the birth of a deer outside my birthplace. I don't know whether something like it is said in other parts of Mexico. The saying had been filed away in my memory, and its image had not bothered me until it was revived by the Kurosawa movie. My interest was spurred by the poetic impact of the foxes' wedding procession through the woods.

Now, in the fresh air outside the movie, I imagined an im-

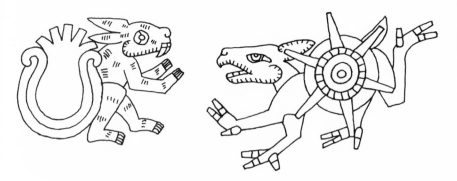

Figure 3. A rabbit carrying the moon and a deer carrying the sun (*Codex Borgia,* p. 33).

mense physiological process in the sky, with a torrential rupture of an amniotic sac between the legs of a gigantic mother. Then I looked between the clouds for her noble son, expelled from her womb, the sun itself. Recalling images portrayed in the Meso-american tradition many centuries ago, I saw the deer in the *Codex Borgia,* carrying the solar disk, and the rabbit that accompanied him, carrying the moon (fig. 3). In my imagination's improbable sky, a sky of light and rain, of the present and the remote past, the deer was giving birth to the sun in a brief moment of liberation in which the aquatic, dark principles of her pregnant womb coexisted with the luminous, warm principles of new solar life.

Was there a similar relationship at some time between the proverb about birth and the mythical birth of a Sun-Deer? It is quite unlikely. The image of the gigantic mother was merely my imaginary creation. That does not mean, however, that there might not be interesting relationships between sayings and myths, or between this particular saying and some myth. Sayings come from many places. They can come from forgotten anec-dotes or, more seriously, from historical happenings, more func-tionally, from attempts to instruct, and more maliciously, from double meanings. When speaking of earthly events, reference to the great machinery of the universe is also important.

Michel Graulich, an expert on ancient Nahua religion, has emphasized that the solar paradigm existed in many sayings referring to human life and to political institutions. That is why, the Belgian author points out, the ancient Nahua said that an old man's sun was setting, that a mature man was like a sun at its zenith, that a woman who was being married "had found her sun," that a sovereign's election meant that the sun was rising, that a reign without glory was a day with weak sunlight, and that the death of a ruler left the world in darkness.[1]

Sometimes historical sources explain the sayings. An example is *moxoxolotitlani,* an expression that can be translated as "the pages were sent." This saying was used when someone was sent on a errand and didn't accomplish it. Bernardino de Sahagún writes in the *Historia general de las cosas de Nueva España* that the saying came from the time when Quetzalcoatl was the ruler of Tula. The austere ruler found out that women were bathing in his private pool. He sent some messengers, or pages, to find out who the women were, but the agents stayed to watch the bathers and did not return with the information. Quetzalcoatl sent another page with the same result: the messenger remained to look at the women. Quetzalcoatl did not send anyone else.[2]

Was that account a legend? Or was it part of a myth? It is hard to find out. Often, with the passage of centuries, myths and sayings, originally intertwined, followed different paths, and the sayings outlived the myths, even though their senselessness often puzzled children. But that did not always happen, and sometimes it is possible to find relationships in a straightforward manner. Today, among the Trique of Copala, when a woman asks a neighbor for fire, she is said to be an opossum.[3] The saying un-

---

1 Graulich, *Mitos y rituales del México antiguo,* p. 79.

2 Sahagún, *Historia general de las cosas de Nueva España,* vol. 1, book 6, chapter 61, pp. 442–43.

3 Hollembach, "El mundo animal en el folklore de los triques de Copala," p. 455.

doubtedly comes from the myth in which an opossum went to the world of the gods to steal fire, which he later brought to earth.

Speaking of opossums, there is a saying whose meaning, on more than one occasion, must have disturbed the people who used it. Someone who is too cunning is said to be a *chucha cuerera* (leathery bitch). In some parts of Mexico, *chucho* means dog, but it isn't easy to find a reason for calling any kind of dog "leathery." Francisco J. Santamaría explained in his *Diccionario de mejicanismos,* which was based on the *Diccionario geográfico de las Indias Occidentales y América* by Antonio de Alcedo, that *chucha cuerera* was not a bitch but a type of opossum, the *zorra mochilera,* which was highly valued for its hide.[4] Santamaría included some examples of how the expression was used, including the following verses from Vicente T. Mendoza's collection of folklore:

> Even the old maids
> make sure of one thing,
> that they are as good as
> the young single girls,
> and [cleverly] like *chuchas cuereras*
> spend whatever it takes . . .

The meaning is clear (that is, the women are as clever as the opossum). And the opossum is known to be one of the most cunning of all animals. Among other things, it is known for its ability to feign death when it is pursued. Myths, of course, use the opossum's reputation for astuteness to make it one of their favorite characters.

There is an interesting relationship between another saying and a cosmological image that comes from ancient times. The complementary images of the sun and the moon, of the deer

---

4 Santamaría, *Diccionario de mejicanismos,* p. 423.

and the rabbit, were reproduced in an old Nahuatl saying recorded in Sahagún's documents. According to the source, when young people left home and would not obey their fathers or mothers, when they had no fixed residence and would not listen to advice and counsel, they were reprimanded as follows: "You have made yourself into a rabbit, you have made yourself a deer. You have made yourself into a fugitive, you have become hardened. You have taken the rabbit's path, the deer's path."[5] In ancient times, the [metaphorical] names of the eternal astral travelers designated vagabonds, people without home or repose, people who traveled the roads night and day.

I presented these ideas to Martha Rosario. I hoped she would agree, even tentatively, with my unprovable hypothesis about the deer giving birth. But after a long silence, instead of agreeing with me, as I expected, she posed a new question. She asked, "And why do we say in the north, when cold chills our bones, 'Is the crane flapping its wings?'"

5 Sahagún, *Historia general,* vol. 1, book 6, chapter 43, pp. 461–62.

{8}

An Amazing Fruit

It would be easy to call chocolate an amazing fruit. Today, chocolate's dark body dominates the world of gluttony. Chocolate, like the ancient gods of the Mesoamericans, is both lovable and terrible. It is a blessing to the palate, a source of energy, and one of the greatest causes of obesity in industrialized countries. Its daily consumption hasn't made it a vulgar substance. Even with the standardization of its flavors, it is a common luxury—and it is an exquisite luxury for people with refined tastes.

Chocolate has always been an obligatory topic for nutritionists and gastronomists, but now it is also one for economists. Today, when business values are king, the production of chocolate is important to the world economy. Paradoxically, the economic potential of this American fruit was not perceived by the first Spaniards who wrote about it. To the contrary, the fruit was considered a symbol of an idyllic time when precious metals did not dominate peoples' relationships.

Francisco Hernández, Philip II's royal physician (*protomédico*), writing about the *cacahuacuahuitl,* or cacao tree, in his monumental work *Historia natural de Nueva España,* stated as much.[1] "It brings to mind," Hernández said, "the great stages of human his-

---

1 Hernández, vol. 2, book 6, chapter 87, pp. 303–305.

tory," referring to the primitive times when goods were not sold for gold or silver, but, as Homer sang, were bartered. Hernández's romantic vision even denied the existence of greed and ambition in the New World before the arrival of his compatriots, who brought money to the conquered lands. The *protomédico* said that in the New World, people used the feathers of beautiful birds, cotton cloth, precious stones, and especially the *cacahuatl,* or chocolate seed, as money.

Hernández found in chocolate another reason to distinguish between the materialistic present of the New World and its imaginary idyllic past. He said that although wild grapevines grew in the jungles of the conquered, the Indians had not learned how to make wine, and that they used chocolate to prepare a nourishing drink with a pleasant flavor and diverse medical uses.

It was precisely chocolate's diversity that astonished the Spaniards. They attributed to it such a variety of physiological effects and nutritional benefits, as well as harm to the body, that the composition of the fruit itself was a marvel according to the Hippocratic criteria used at that time. They thought that when chocolate was eaten without being toasted or pretreated, it constipated, stopped menstruation and urination, obstructed the liver and the spleen, drained color from people's faces, weakened digestion, shortened the breath, and caused paroxysms and fainting spells, malfunction of the uterus (*mal de madre*), a continuous anxiety, melancholy, irregular heartbeats, and, in some people, swelling and dropsy. On the other hand, the Spaniards said that toasted and ground chocolate, with no other additive than a little corn gruel, was a healthy food that nourished and fattened people, gave a good appetite, helped digestion, produced urine, cured *mal de madre,* brought happiness, and strengthened the body.

Juan de Cárdenas, another doctor in New Spain, tried to solve the mystery of the contradictory properties of chocolate and devoted a good part of his 1591 book to that topic. The book was called *Problemas y secretos maravillosos de las Indias (Marvelous Prob-*

lems and Secrets of the Indies).[2] Cárdenas wrote that chocolate was composed of at least three different substances. The first substance was cold, dry, thick, terrestrial, and melancholic, very dangerous to the organism, harsh and astringent, what he called "chocolate earth." The second substance was of a gaseous nature, oily, warm, and wet in character, and fatty and buttery in flavor; its effect was bland, soothing, and gentle. The third substance was fiery because it was very hot and penetrating. It was characterized by the slightly bitter taste of green cacao, and it caused headaches. But because it was also sharp, light, and penetrating, it was the reason for the "opening-up" properties of chocolate that induced perspiration, menstruation, and bowel movements. Because of this, chocolate was classified by the medical criteria of the time as a product with contrary features: cold and dry in its terrestrial part, hot and wet in its oily part, and warm and dry in its light, bitter part. Its predominant nature, however, was cold and dry.

Many other Spanish doctors dealt with the puzzle of chocolate. Antonio Colmenero de Ledesma, a surgeon in the city of Ecija, published his *Curioso tratado de la naturaleza y calidad del chocolate* in 1631.[3] This work launched the reputation of chocolate in Europe, a reputation that puzzled scholars, conquered palates, and increased the repertoire of doctors.

Chocolate had amazed members of the ancient native societies as well. The Nahua forbade its consumption by commoners. Those who violated the law were executed. This is why it could be referred to by the metaphor "heart, blood." They also said it was nutritious ("cold," according to the ancient concepts), and that if the fruit were eaten green and in large quantities it could cause serious intoxication.[4]

2 Cárdenas (book 2, chapters 7–9, pp. 176–94) deals extensively with properties of chocolate.

3 Colmenero de Ledesma, *Chocolate, or, an Indian Drink.*

4 On Nahua concepts about chocolate, see *Florentine Codex* (book 6, p. 256; book 11, p. 119) and *Códice Florentino* (book 6, fol. 211v–212r; book 11, fol. 123r).

In brief, the ancient texts said that chocolate was expensive, dangerous (*imacaxoni*), likely to produce fright (*tetzammachoya*), enervating, very nutritious, and cold. These attributes were not all independent. In native thought they were interrelated, and they placed chocolate among the things of this world that were heavy and contaminated with death. In order to understand that idea better, we must remember that in Mesoamerica it was believed that earthly things had a dual nature. All of them, human beings, animals, plants, minerals, manufactured objects, were composed of two kinds of matter: one light, internal, and invisible, the other a sheath, heavy and visible. Even the gods were encased in heavy matter when they came to this world. The heavy matter restricted the actions of bodies and linked them with death.

A parallel idea exists today. The loss of the light matter will increase a body's solidity. Maarten Jansen says that when the Mixtec of Chalcatongo cut down a tree, they try to prevent the escape of its *anu* (soul). They believe that if the *anu* is kept inside the tree, the wood will continue to be soft and will be easier to split.[5]

We can see the opposition between heavy and light matter in a story about a magicians' expedition in the time of the ruler (*tlatoani*) Motecuhzoma Ilhuicamina.[6] The tale also mentions the heaviness of chocolate. The Mexica ruler sought the opinion of his co-ruler, Tlacaelel, about the advisability of sending an embassy to Culhuacan-Chicomoztoc, the mythical place of origin of the Mexica and their patron god, Huitzilopochtli. The messengers were to search for Coatlicue, the mother of the god, and give her greetings from her son and the Mexica. Tlacaelel agreed with Motecuhzoma Ilhuicamina, and, as the old official historian documents extensively, they searched for sixty elderly magicians to undertake the journey.

---

5 Jansen, *Huisi tacu: Estudio interpretativo de un libro mixteco antiguo,* vol. 1, p. 136.
6 Durán, *The History of the Indies of New Spain,* pp. 212–22.

The old men left loaded with valuable gifts. When they arrived at Coatepec they stopped, covered their bodies with the ointments of their profession, prayed, and were transformed into birds and wild beasts in order to reach Culhuacan-Chicomoztoc. They arrived at a large lake with the hill of Culhuacan in its middle. The magicians reverted to their human shape and went to the island by canoe. Some fishermen who spoke Nahuatl, as the magicians did, asked what they were there for. The magicians answered that they were Mexica in search of their ancestors' land. The old servant of the goddess Coatlicue came forth to greet them. When the magicians introduced themselves as envoys from Motecuhzoma and Tlacaelel, the old man said he didn't know who those individuals were because the leaders who had gone forth from Chicomoztoc centuries before had been others. Then he named the guides for that migration. The magicians said that they knew those names historically, but that they were men who had died long ago. The old man was surprised at that information. He asked, "Who killed them? Because all the people they left in this place are still alive. No one here has died."

After a long conversation, the old man told the magicians to follow him to the place where Coatlicue was. They followed him as he easily climbed up the slope. The magicians, on the other hand, first sank up to their knees in the sand and later sank up to their waists. The old man asked, "Mexica, what is going on? What makes you so heavy? What do you eat on earth?"

They had to answer, "Master, we eat the food that grows there, and we drink chocolate."

The old man said to them, "Sons, those meals you eat and the drinks you consume make you solid and heavy and will not allow you to go to see the place where your ancestors lived. That is what caused your death."

Afterward, he took one of their loads on his shoulders, climbed up with it as if it were a straw, and then returned for all the other loads.

The story went on to tell about the magicians' arrival before the goddess, the delivery of their message, and the reply given to them, a new reprimand for drinking chocolate. It told about their return after again being transformed into birds and beasts, and about the disappearance of twenty of them during their conversion back to their human bodies.

The text clearly divided space into two different dimensions. In the place of myth, beings go on forever. In the human world they are contaminated with death. Humans have no choice except to consume the products of their environment, but those products contain the heavy matter that leads to death. Among those foods, the most nutritious are the heaviest. The most valuable one is that amazing chocolate.

{9}
The Miracle of the Eagle and the Cactus

When the god Huitzilopochtli guided his people to the promised land, he punished his sister Malinalxochitl, the evil sorceress, for her excesses.[1] She and her group were left on the road while the other pilgrims continued their march to the lake region. Malinalxochitl's son, Copil, wanted to avenge his mother, and he attacked the Mexica as they arrived at Chapultepec, but he was defeated. His head was placed at the top of Tepetzinco, and his heart was thrown into Lake Tetzcoco among the reeds and canebrakes. Thirty-nine years later, in the year 1-Tecpatl (1324), the leaders Cuauhtlequetzqui and Axolohua returned to the place where Copil's heart had sunk, and there they saw the miracle of the eagle that Huitzilopochtli had said would signal the end of his people's journey.

This lesson about patriotic symbols begins with the story of a miracle. The national emblem recalls the arrival and island settlement of a group of people in the lake's basin. The name and fame of those people were used to create our Mexican identity, and the island where Mexico-Tenochtitlan was founded atop Copil's mythical heart was to become the heart of the country. As the image of the sun god was emblazoned on the center of the flag, the symbol took on a single meaning, and the story of the miracle became officially restricted to only one of its versions.

1 Durán, *The History of the Indies of New Spain,* pp. 31–41.

Like all symbols, that of the eagle perched on a cactus to devour a serpent continued to yield new interpretations that became increasingly farther removed from those of the people who originally described the miracle in the context of a long-gone cosmovision. As a child, I was taught that the gallant and majestic eagle on the flag embodied all the patriotic virtues, and the serpent, all the vices. Virtue destroyed vice by tearing its body apart with its iron beak. The image had been converted into a moral allegory, designed to touch children's hearts. The allegory went even further when the image was reworked and brought up to date to symbolize Mexico's twentieth-century anti-imperialist stance. Alfonso Caso stated it thus:

> Mexico is not now, nor ever will be, an imperialist country. Our mission is not like that of the Romans or the Aztecs to rule over other countries, but instead to live in peace with them. . . . The eagle and the cactus on our banner continue to be our inspiration. We still believe, as the Aztecs did, that it is fundamental that lives be guided by ideals, and those ideals can only be to work together to ensure that good is triumphant. Thus, the old symbol that motivated the Aztecs to cross the northern deserts and plains, until they established the City of the Sun in the middle of the Lake of the Moon is still alive. It continues to fuel our desire to create a great nation that has its center where the eagle stood on the cactus for the first time.[2]

Now, long after the cosmological vision that created it has disappeared, the elements of the symbol have acquired another meaning. Today we emphasize the devouring action of the eagle as if it were the emblem's primary meaning. The eagle and the serpent were indeed oppositionally paired in Mesoamerican symbolism, but that opposition was not the key to the miracle in

2 Caso, "El aguila y el nopal."

the foundation of Mexico-Tenochtitlan. It was subsumed under the main symbolic opposition in the image, that of the eagle and the cactus. Accounts of the miracle, tying myth to a historical event, will show us the importance of the eagle/cactus opposition—and the existence of a pact between two leaders.

People who live immersed in symbolism see its presence everywhere. Every nook is a microcosm, every murmur a transcendent message, every event a metaphor. For believers, reality ratifies the cosmic formula, and every important event must fit the consecrated model. The Mesoamericans followed this pattern. In traditional societies, events must fit the canonical plan in order to acquire their full meaning. History must be interpreted within the confines of the sacred. The Mexica, immersed in that concept of the world and of society, developed a historiography in which events, in order to be authentic, to be legitimate, had to be clothed in myth and miracle.

In the story of the origin of Mexico-Tenochtitlan, the political reality of the moment had to be coordinated with a symbol of the binary opposition between water and fire—an important image for all Mesoamerican people and one used by many of them as a fundamental symbol. In Mexico-Tenochtitlan, as in other political-religious centers, the opposition of water and fire was embodied in the main temple-pyramid, on top of which were two chapels, one dedicated to the sun god and to war, the other to Tlaloc, the god of rain. The union of the two opposites symbolized the agreement of the founders.

The original population of Mexico-Tenochtitlan was composed of several groups, each of whom had traveled under the guidance of a chief who embodied power and who bore the name of the group's patron god.[3] During the migration, serious

---

3 The chiefs of the *calpultin,* or migrant groups, were described in the sources as human-gods, that is, humans possessed by a god, who carried both the god's image and his name. See the example of Cuauhtlequetzqui (López Austin, *Hombre-dios,* pp. 114, 121).

conflicts had arisen among the leaders, and the tensions did not end after the travelers settled the lake's islands. These conflicting interests had to be accommodated. Some historical accounts imply that the establishment of the city was owing to a compromise between two of the principal leaders. As was customary, the pact was expressed in the form of a symbol. The transaction and the cosmic model became merged in the miracle; the compromise was represented in the city's name and in its religious symbol.

The final deal was made between the Cuauhtlequetzqui (He Who Raises the Eagle's Fire), also called Cuauhcoatl (Eagle-like Serpent or Serpent-Eagle), and the guide Tenoch (Rock Cactus or Hard Cactus, the name of a cactus species).[4] According to the historian Chimalpahin Cuauhtlehuanitzin, both chiefs were represented in the miracle, no doubt because they saw in it, united in a hierophany of opposites, the two gods they incarnated, one fiery and solar, the other aquatic. Referring to the site where Copil's heart had sunk, Cuauhtlequetzqui said to Tenoch:

> At that place Cópil's heart will germinate, and you will go there to watch and keep vigil when a tenuchtli [rock cactus] sprouts from Cópil's heart, and you will lie in wait for the precise moment an eagle stands on top of the cactus, holding tightly in its claws a half upright serpent, which he will be mauling, wishing to devour it, while it hisses and whistles. And when this appears, Tenuché, because you are that, the Tenuch, the Cactus with the Hard Red Prickly Pear, and the eagle you will see, Tenuché, that eagle will be me. Me myself, with my lips bloodied by what I am devouring, because that will be me, Cuauhtlequetzqui. . . . Then the prophecy will come to pass that no one in the world will ever be able to destroy or erase the glory, the honor and the fame of Mexico-Tenochtitlan.[5]

4 Hernández, in *Historia natural de Nueva España* (vol. 2, p. 313), described this species of cactus as "a plant resembling the cacuts in its flowers and fruit, but with long, thin, twisted stalks."

5 Chimalpahin Cuauhtlehuanitzin, *Relaciones originales de Chalco Amaquemecan*, p. 55.

Figure 4. The eagle on a cactus (*Codex Mendoza,* pl. 1, fol. 2r).

The agreement was symbolized in the name of the city itself. It was the place of Mexi, the fire god, and also of the aquatic god Tenoch.

Chimalpahin Cuauhtlehuanitzin's account mentions the serpent, but not all versions of the tale do so. With this in mind, we will apply to the images of this union the methodology proposed by Lévi-Strauss for understanding myths. There has never been an in-depth study of the cosmic significance of the solar eagle, and we cannot do it here. We will, however, compare the known classical versions.

The serpent does not appear in all of the texts that describe the miracle or in all of its representations in pictures or sculptures. The eagle is shown eating a bird, clutching a human heart,

Figure 5. The eagle eating a serpent on a cactus (Durán 1994: vol. 1, tract 1, pl. 3, chap. 5, p. 21).

holding the symbol of war with his beak, or simply perched on the cactus with an empty beak (figs. 4–7). That does not mean that the serpent was merely incidental in the iconographic concept. In order to find its symbolic value, however, we must analyze the images that replace it in other representations.

Let us examine versions of two marvelous visions that omit the serpent. Here are two texts from Durán:

> Thus they continued to roam from one place to another, seeking one that would be suitable as a permanent home. And wandering this way, among the reeds and rushes, they came upon a beautiful spring and saw wondrous things in the waters. These things had been predicted to the people by their priests, through the command of Huitzilopochtli, their god.
>
> The first thing they beheld was a white bald cypress, all white and very beautiful, and the spring came forth from the foot of the tree.
>
> The second thing they saw was a group of white willows around the spring, without a single green leaf.
>
> There were white reeds, and white rushes surrounding the water.

Figure 6. The eagle eating a bird on a cactus. (Durán 1994: vol. 2, tract 1, pl. 32, chap. 74, p. 348).

Figure 7. Relief on the Mexica monolith called the Teocalli (temple) of the Sacred War, rear view (National Museum of Anthropology, Mexico City).

White frogs came out of the water, white fish came out, white water snakes, all shiny and white.

The spring flowed out from between two large rocks, the water so clear and limpid that it was pleasing to behold. The priests and elders, remembering what their god had told them, wept with joy and became exuberant, crying out:

We have now found the promised land. We have now seen the relief, the happiness of the weary Aztec people. All we desired has come true.[6]

6 Durán, *History,* pp. 40–41.

Thus they again found the spring they had seen the day before. But the water on that day had been clear and transparent, and now it flowed out in two streams, one red, like blood, and the other so blue and thick that it filled the people with awe. Having seen these mysterious things [where the red and blue waters flowed as one], the Aztecs continued to seek [the omen of] the eagle whose presence had been foretold. Wandering from one place to another, they soon discovered the prickly pear cactus. On it stood the eagle with his wings stretched out toward the rays of the sun, basking in its warmth and the freshness of the morning. In his talons he held a bird with very fine feathers, precious and shining. When the people saw the eagle they humbled themselves, making reverences as if the bird were a divine thing. The eagle, seeing them, also humbled himself, bowing his head low in their direction.[7]

Mexico-Tenochtitlan began with a miracle. This was not a unique event in Mesoamerican history. The gods appeared in a marvelous vision every time it was necessary to found, repopulate, or narrate the origin of an important site. The *Relación de Michoacán,* for instance, gives a beautiful description of how the Tarasca priests discovered the gods' presence among the crags of the site where they would built Pátzcuaro.[8] A second example is Chiconcuac, a town near Mexico City, that was dedicated to the corn goddess. That is why its name meant "Chicomecoatl's Place" and why the name of the goddess meant "7-Serpent." The story was that in 1272, a person named Cuahuitzatzin saw a trickle of smoke that looked like a rainbow emerge from some big reeds. Following it, he came upon an enormous serpent whose sides were painted in seven colors, the incarnation of the goddess.[9]

We Mexicans have taken the founding of a Mesoamerican

7 Durán, *History,* pp.43–44.
8 *Relación de las ceremonias y ritos . . .,* part 2, chapter 6, pp. 34–35.
9 Chimalpahin Cuauhtlehuanitzin, *Relaciones originales,* pp. 134–35.

city as a national symbol. To be entirely correct, we have adopted one of the versions of the event. We select, we establish, we remythologize. And we want to remythologize. Above all else, we want to renew the myth when we look at the urban blot of Mexico City, grown beyond all logic, beyond all human dimension. The place where Copil's heart was sunk continues to grow as if impelled by Malinalxochitl's malignant curse.

10

The Eclipse

The moon, accompanied by the inaudible music of the spheres and flaunting the blackest of her masks, was the celestial actress in an unusual event, a marvelous free spectacle that took place on July 11, 1991. People living inside the fortuitous band of darkness attended the gala event. Many sought aesthetic pleasure in it. A few added science to their pleasure. Others brought atavistic fears, reflected in the eyes of pregnant mothers.

Once again the coupling of the human and the celestial domains makes the looming shadow an omen of disaster. It has always been that way. Misfortune and eclipse were associated with Nero's matricide in   59, with the Black Plague that devastated Europe beginning in 1348, with the terrible hurricanes in the West Indies in 1791, with Napoleon III's war against Prussia in 1870, and with thousands of other events. Such associations will probably continue until the end of humankind.

Sources record how Mesoamericans of the Postclassic period feared eclipses. Friar Bernardino de Sahagún's texts relate what the ancient Nahua believed about solar and lunar eclipses: that a pregnant woman should not look at one or expose herself to its influence, because if she did, her child could be turned into a mouse or be born with a harelip, a cut nose, twisted lips, cross-eyes, a twisted face, or a monstrous or imperfect body. To prevent the harm, the woman had to place a piece of obsidian in her mouth or on her belly.[1] Sahagún's documents said this about the eclipse of the sun in particular:

> When this occurs [the sun] turns red. It is no longer quiet, no longer tranquil. It is only balancing itself. There is immediate turmoil. People are restless, there is an uproar, fear and weeping. People wail, give cries of alarm, scream, clamor, rattle hawk bells. Albinos are sacrificed. Captives are sacrificed. People shed their own blood, piercing their ears with reeds, and flowery songs are sung in the temples. The noise continues, the wailing persists. It was said, "If it comes to an end, if the Sun is eaten, everything will become dark forever. The [feminine monsters called] *tzitzimime* will come down to devour the people."[2]

In San Pedro Chenalhó, in May 1953, Manuel Arias Sojom told Calixta Guiteras Holmes a rich sample of Tzotzil beliefs. Some of them seem to echo the ancient fears of the Nahua on the high Central Plateau of Mexico. Arias Sojom said,

> The eclipse is called *poslob.* It shows us what the moon's death would be like. If the moon dies, many women will also die. Men weep, thinking about their wives and their daughters. Women cry even more. I have seen my mother crying, kneeling, praying, while we pounded sticks and boards, making a great noise. We stopped pounding when the moon came out again. . . .
> My father's mother was still living one time when the sun stopped. It was *poslob,* and it looked like a star. It happened on a Saturday. The *chojchojotro* were coming to take out men's and women's eyes,[3] but everyone had covered his eyelids with wax

---

1 *Florentine Codex,* book 5, chapter 15, pp. 189–90; book 7, chapter 2, pp. 8–9.

2 *Códice Florentino,* book 7, chapter 1, fol. 1v, López Austin translation.

3 Arias Sojom did not describe the *chojchojotro,* but they have been described elsewhere as eagles or large hawks, related to destructive forces and eclipses (Guitera Holmes, *Los peligros del alma: Visión del mundo de un tzotzil,* p. 272).

from virgin honey, and that was what the *chojchojotro* found. That
was how they protected their eyes.[4]

Fear can be the source of great creations. Since ancient times
fear of eclipses has motivated humans to observe the sky. In
China there were sages devoted to observing the paths and inci-
dents of astral bodies. One of the three classic books in which
the oldest of written Chinese literature appears, the *Shu Jing*
(*Book of the History*), mentions an eclipse that took place on October 22, 2137   In Mesoamerica, the Maya of the Classic period, whose arithmetical system allowed them to manage large
numbers, were able to correlate cycles of different periods and to
predict solar eclipses. On pages 51 to 58 of the *Dresden Codex*
there is a sequence of 405 consecutive lunations covering a period of nearly 33 years. The lunations were divided into 69
groups the ends of which were the days when, in some part of
the earth, a solar eclipse might occur. The Maya did not know
this fact, but they did know that any solar eclipse visible in their
territory would happen on one of those dates.

The Maya's mathematical calculations were more advanced
than those of other Mesoamericans. They rejected the idea that
the darkening of the sun was haphazard, converting the event
into a mathematical regularity. With the development of the
lunation tables, solar eclipses were no longer celestial accidents
but magnificent events governed by a universal law that sages
could understand. The ability to predict eclipses, however, did
not overcome their fear. It simply helped the Maya priests to
avert, in a timely manner, the misfortunes attributed to the sun's
blackout.

Fear of cataclysms, wars, diminished crops, deaths of rulers,
malformations, cross-eyed children with harelips—at first, native
beliefs may give the impression that, in traditional thought, dis-

4 Guiteras Holmes, *Los peligros del alma,* p. 138.

parate ideas can accumulate with no rhyme or reason and, being readily accepted by the people, lead to a heap of superstition. The matter was not that simple. The secular persistence of these ideas should make us suspect that there were fundamental, if unconscious, reasons for coherence among believers in a particular cosmovision. Even if they could not perceive the structural basis of their culture, they expected the supernatural to be explicable. Mere faith was not enough; they looked for rational reasons for their beliefs.

Thus, in Manuel Arias Sojom's words we see an attempt to explain supernatural processes. For example, he dealt with the belief that a child would be cross-eyed if its mother looked directly at the full moon while pregnant, saying that her eyes were simultaneously attracted by two side-by-side luminous sources, the full moon and the ocote pine torch.[5] According to him, cross-eyes were caused by the mother's effort to look in both directions at once, an effect transmitted to the child.

Perhaps the reason given by Arias Sojom would be insufficient in another, more complex cosmovision with more numerous and intricate relationships, but it is a good example of the search for cause and effect in an area of knowledge in which many researchers have denied that any kind of logical explanation exists. Some scholars say that in the world of beliefs, only faith produces certainty. Such statements frequently arise from a total lack of anthropological knowledge. Beliefs are built on more solid foundations, with logic based on a coherent body of thought and refined as time goes by. Even we nonbelievers who study religious thought as outsiders can find congruence in cosmovisions that are alien to us.

In Mesoamerica, one of the principal harmful effects attributed to eclipses was the harelip. The belief probably came from the widely held concept that a harelip was produced by the ac-

5 Guiteras Holmes, *Los peligros del alma,* p. 99.

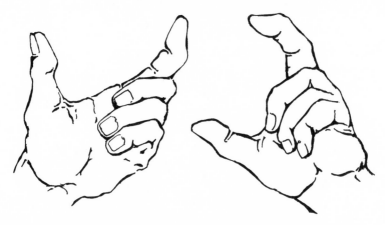

Figure 8. Hand positions used by the Achí to indicate the seasons. *Left:* dry season, the moon is vertical to hold water. *Right:* rainy season, moon on its side to spill water (from Neuenswander 1981).

tion of a luminous lunar substance that had spilled over the earth from on high.

The moon was a container. This is clearly shown in the ancient pictographic codices, which portray the vessel in cross-section with a liquid content. In some images a rabbit or sometimes a flint knife sits on top of the liquid. As a container, the moon both holds and releases. It retains when it is solid. It is empty when it gives off almost no light. It retains in the dry season; it spills out in the rainy season.

The moon's characteristics as a container are also shown by the hand signs of the modern Achí (fig. 8). According to Neuenswander, the Achí indicate the dry season by a position of the hand that refers to a massive moon, full of liquid, like a container in a vertical position. The same position of the fingers, but with the hand turned, signifies the rainy season. The moon turns over to allow its contents to spill.[6]

6 Neuenswander, "Vestiges of Early Maya Time Concepts in a Contemporary Maya (Cubulco Achí) Community: Implications for Epigraphy."

A Tenejapa myth tells that the moon does not shine as brightly as the sun because it is a body that empties itself, that weeps.[7] The moon releases its liquid, which is light, which is crying, which is rain. That is the reason why, in many native beliefs, earthly beings, trees, intestinal worms, harvests, domestic animals, and even human beings contain a smaller or a greater amount of water according to the phases of the moon. For people who believe in these lunar attributes, there are logical practical consequences. For example, it is not a good idea to cut down a tree when its trunk is filled with water.

During the new moon, the invisible liquid floods the earth. It is composed of many essences. One of them that is terrible for a developing fetus is the rabbit essence. If the rabbit essence penetrates a pregnant woman's womb, her child will be possessed and will show it on his upper lip, which will resemble that of the being who invaded it.

There is a problem in determining exactly what causes the harelip—the lunar liquid or the eclipse itself. The bottom line is that the harm comes from the liquid, but the means are the strong irradiations on the eyes of the pregnant woman or the spilling of the liquid on the earth's surface. Texts about ancient Nahua beliefs show that even without an eclipse, harmful effects could be produced merely by a pregnant woman's glancing at the brilliant face of the moon.

> Pregnant women, when their infants were still not well-formed, were prevented from looking upward, to look to where the Moon comes out. They said to them, "Don't look at the Moon. Your children will be sickly or will have a harelip.[8]

An eclipse of the moon represented a violent, extraordinary rupture, which for a moment stopped the full moon in order to

7 Girón Gómez, "El Sol y la Luna."
8 *Códice Florentino,* book 5, chapter 19, fol. 20r, López Austin translation.

Figure 9. The moon goddess with a rabbit on her lap. Late Classic Maya vessel in the American Museum of Natural History, New York City (Schele and Miller 1986: pl. 120, p. 308).

spill its liquid, in one stroke, over the earth. An eclipse of the sun was the momentary domination of the sun by the empty moon, which diminished or negated the solar light's contrary and equalizing power over the earth. Eclipses injected a large quantity of lunar liquid into worldly beings, either because the water-light of the full moon spilled all at once during the lunar eclipse or because, during a solar eclipse, the water-light that spilled during the full moon was strengthened by the weakening of the opposing force of the sun. In either case, the rabbit takes possession of weaker beings, those who are just being formed.

Is it possible that the ancient Maya had, among the fears that impelled them to explore the realm of celestial regularities, a fear of the lunar rabbit's influence? There is no way of knowing whether they had a myth similar to that of the Nahua of the Central Plateau. According to the Nahua, the sun and the moon were born with equal luminous potential. The gods, who did not think it fair for the two bodies to be equal, darkened the face of one of them by striking its face with a rabbit. In chapter 1 I stated that myths did not generate beliefs about the relationships among the different beings of the cosmos. To the contrary, it was the belief in those relationships that produced the myths. Therefore, the relationship between the rabbit and the moon's diminished light was told in antiquity, and it continues to be told in our own time, not in a single mythical story but as numerous divine adventures, different one from the other.

We know that the ancient Maya believed in a relationship between the rabbit and the moon. Scenes taken from divine adventures appear on the sides of Mayan vessels. We know little about those myths because the scenes were set images from a long story that has not come down to us through other sources. There are times, however, when the association among the characters is quite clear—for example, the association between the moon goddess and the rabbit. In the American Museum of Natural History in New York there is a beautiful, incised, cylindrical ceramic vase dating to the late Classic period (between   550 and 800). The scene depicted on it is quite complex. It shows three figures at the entrance to the underworld, climbing up the cosmic tree, along with a mythical being who is playing music on a conch shell, the jaws of the Celestial Monster, who is spitting out the coiled body of an enormous serpent, and, in the upper part of the vase, the serene figure of the moon goddess (fig. 9). The goddess, straddling the moon glyph—a broad, curved figure that is a true vessel—holds in her lap a happy rabbit.

11

The Antichrist
and the Suns

Its immense, terrible profile cast a shadow over the sky. It was a double apocalyptic beast that emerged, first from the sea, then from the earth, seducing humans with celestial fire: "Then I saw a wild beast come out of the sea with ten horns and seven heads, and on its horns were ten diadems, and on its heads blasphemous names. The beast I saw was like a leopard, but it had paws like a bear and the mouth of a lion. The dragon gave it his own power and throne, together with great authority" (Rev. 13:1–2). "Then I saw another wild beast come up out of the earth; it had two horns like a ram and it spoke like a dragon. It used the authority of the first beast to promote its interests by making the world and all its inhabitants worship the first beast, whose mortal wound had been healed" (Rev. 13:11–12).

The idea of the Antichrist was the product of several influences. One was Persian and Babylonian influence upon Jewish thought. From it came the concept of the battle that would take place between Good and Evil at the end of the world. That concept, united with the Jewish passion for liberty, resulted in terrible prophecies: the first and older one is found in the Book of Daniel, whose Beast has been interpreted as the tyrant Antioch IV Epiphanes. Then Revelation was written, and the beasts represented Rome and its empire during a period of violent persecutions of the emerging church. The Second Epistle to the

Thessalonians (2 Thess. 2) spoke about the rule of the Lawless One as the sad prologue to the Second Coming of Christ. Then, in the Epistles of Saint John, the Antichrist appeared under that name (1 John 2:18–22 and 2 John).

Over the course of history, colorful popular knowledge, theological interpretations, and important proselytizing works were added to this tradition: the so-called Sibylline prophecies. The concept of the Antichrist complemented those of the Second Coming of Christ and the Millennium. Christ's forces had been attacked by Evil. The dominion of Evil would increase in the future until a ruler belonging to the devil appeared. This ruler's reign would be brief, because Christ's armies would overthrow him in the decisive last battle fought on earth, Armageddon. After the triumph of the forces of Good, the last thousand years of the world's existence would be the reign of the saints, and all of humanity would be blessed. A new and definitive Jerusalem would be established. The monsters of the Apocalypse would be included in the penultimate moment of that great final drama. The dragon represented the devil, and the double beast represented the Antichrist, the ruler who served the devil.

The idea of the Antichrist appears and reappears throughout history. It is usually tied to periods of crisis when desperation leads to millenarianism. The terrible figure is blurred, and the devil is not always clearly identified. The Antichrist has been imagined to be a human being, but also as an abstraction, the personification of error and apostasy. As a man he has been pictured as handsome, seductive, and possessing immense knowledge, but he has also been portrayed as a demon or a flying dragon. In one of the visions of Saint Hildegard of Bingen in the twelfth century, the Antichrist had a monstrous black head, inflamed eyes, donkey's ears, and a belly with a great open mouth with iron teeth.

Because he was a vague figure opposing the forces of faith, politicians of many stripes have been able to identify their worst enemies as the Antichrist. Frederick I Barbarossa was identified as the Antichrist by some. Popes Boniface VIII and John XXII were named as the Beast—and so were all the rest of the papacy, by Luther. Luther himself was so identified when attacked by Muntzer, his former admirer.

This attribution has also been applied collectively and has led to intolerance and fanaticism. In the second century there was an early prediction that the Antichrist would be a Jew from the Dan tribe, born in Babylon, reared in Palestine, and accepted by the Jews as the Messiah. The patristic tradition about the Beast was established by Hippolytus, author of a *Treatise on the Antichrist*. In it, the Antichrist was said to be a Jew imitating Christ. Hippolytus, with his *Treatise,* opened the way to identifying all Jews with the evil host. Later, the hordes of the Antichrist became Muslims, or Mongols, or (according to Anabaptists) Lutherans and Catholics.

The theological concept of the Antichrist varied considerably even in the first centuries of Christianity. Clement of Alexandria (150–215) pursued the symmetrical projection of good and evil to the point of setting up, in opposition to the Christian Trinity, a trinity of corruption: the devil was the father, the Antichrist was his son, and the inclination to sin, owing to original sin, was the evil spirit. Origen (184–253), on the other hand, denied the historical reality of the Millennium, stating that it would take place neither in time nor in space but in the souls of the faithful, a concept the church used when, triumphant, it wanted to bar reformist ideas.

The notion of a historical Millennium, however, lay dormant in popular thought. It took on new doctrinal impetus when Lactantius (260–325) taught that the devil had been overthrown by Christ's sacrifice. According to him, the forces of Evil would reorganize and the Antichrist would appear as their leader to defeat the Christian community. After the triumph of Evil, God would again send Christ, the liberator, who, with his angelic hosts, would bring about the Millennium. Commodius (fifth century   ) added that Christ's hosts would be the descendants of the ten lost tribes of Israel, missing until then. Responding to the attack of those armies, the Antichrist would flee toward the north, to return with a powerful army composed of the towns known collectively as Gog and Magog. In the end, he would be defeated and thrown into hell.

Saint Augustine (354–430) considered the Apocalypse to be a spiritual allegory and thought that the Millennium had begun with the triumph of the church. And the debate went on. Many centuries later, the Antichrist was included in one of the most influential Christian theological ideas, the Joaquinist theory of the Three Ages. Joachim of Fiore (1130–1202) divided the history of the world into the ages of the Father, the Son, and the Holy Ghost. According to Joachim, the last era would begin in 1260, and it would have as its sorrowful beginning a brief period of domination by the forces of the Antichrist.

There is no doubt that painful episodes associated with the Crusades, the European peasant wars, and the Reformation gave great impetus to the image of the Antichrist among the populace. At the same time, there emerged the concept of his adversary, the Emperor of the Last Days, who would fight on God's side. Frederick I Barbarossa was the Antichrist for his adversaries, but for his followers he was the heroic Emperor of the Faith.

The Beast's image, shifting, blurry, but always terrible, eventually crossed the ocean and reached lands far removed from Europe in space and in history. Motolinia could compare the flames of the Nicaraguan volcano to the fire that would consume the Antichrist.[1]

Mesoamerican sources mention that the present world emerged after four successive creations and destructions, although they disagree as to their order. Each era bore the name of its dominant

1 Motolinía, *Memoriales*, chapter 68, p. 284.

sun: the one with Tezcatlipoca as its celestial body was called the Sun of Jaguar (Ocelotonatiuh); the one with Quetzalcoatl, the Sun of Wind (Ehecatonatiuh); the one with Tlaloc, the Sun of the Rain of Fire (Tletonatiuh); and the one with the goddess of water, Chalchiuhtlicue, the Sun of Water (Atonatiuh).

Each era came to an end convulsively, one after the other. The names indicated the nature of the cataclysm that led to the following period. The Sun of Jaguar ended when Tezcatlipoca was defeated by Quetzalcoatl, who attacked him with a great club. Tezcatlipoca fell into the water, where he was turned into a jaguar. The nocturnal beast returned to earth to devour its creatures, who were not really humans but giants.

The Sun of Wind ended with Tezcatlipoca's revenge. The god of night climbed up to the sky and with a tremendous kick brought down the reigning Quetzalcoatl. Tezcatlipoca immediately installed the rain god, Tlaloc, or Tlalocantecuhtli, but Quetzalcoatl climbed up to the sky again and caused a terrible rain of fire that ended Tlaloc's dominion.

Then Chalchiuhtlicue, the goddess of water, assumed power. Like those before her, she saw her reign come to an end in a catastrophe, this time an enormous deluge that covered the whole world.

In the end, the land itself, winds, a rain of fire, and floods destroyed the beings that preceded humans. The first group, giants, ate acorns and were destroyed completely by earthquakes, or else were devoured by Tezcatlipoca and his jaguars. The beings of the second sun lived on pine nuts, according to one source, or mesquite, according to others. The winds that blew during the cataclysm at the end of that era were so strong that few survived; those who did, clinging to the branches of trees, were turned into monkeys. The beings of the third sun ate water maize, *acicintli,* and were afflicted by a rain of fire, sand, and stones. This was the time when boiling *tezontle,* volcanic rock, was produced. The rain of fire nearly annihilated the world's inhabitants. The

only ones saved were those who were turned into turkeys, but-
terflies, or dogs. At the end of the fourth sun, the rain was so
heavy that not only did the earth flood but also the skies fell
down. Since then, the survivors of the former beings, who ate
cincocopi, a grain resembling corn, have lived in the water, converted into fish.

Not only does the order of the suns differ among the sources
but so does the duration of each. Usually the number of years
amounted to some multiple of the calendrical cycles. It could
not have been otherwise, because all of creation had profound
calendrical significance. Accordingly, each era had, besides the
name of its dominating sun and its cataclysm, a calendrical name.
The Sun of Jaguar was also called Nahui-Ocelotl (the date 4-
Jaguar); the Sun of Wind, Nahui-Ehecatl (4-Wind); the Sun of
the Rain of Fire, Nahui-Quiahuitl (4-Rain), and the Sun of Water, Nahui-Atl (4-Water). The present era, the fifth sun, was
called Nahui-Ollin (4-Movement), and according to the sources,
it will be destroyed by earthquakes and general starvation. Its end
will be announced precisely at the conclusion of a fifty-two-year
cycle when, the earth exhausted, the sun weakened, human beings will no longer be able to light the fire.

The preceding order is the one given in *Historia de los mexicanos por sus pinturas* and by the monolith called the Aztec Calendar Stone or the Sun Stone. There are four squares on the
central part of the monolith that, read counterclockwise, name
the four preceding eras: Nahui-Ocelotl, Nahui-Ehecatl, Nahui-
Quiahuitl, and Nahui-Atl. A large glyph placed in the center is
the figure of the fifth sun, Nahui-Ollin, armed with claws that
capture hearts.

This Sun Stone was a clear manifestation of the Mesoamerican geometric concept of the universe: the regularity of the
numbers, the exact periodicity of the eras, the alternation of
dominance, the opposition of the gods, the congruence of the
cataclysms, and the use of the center of the monolith's surface as

a solid foundation for the present. The concept of the cosmogonic suns was the result of an attempt to find a global order, a stability, a valid, even if transitory, stability resulting from the succession of alternating forces. The myth of the four suns orders the totality of the creation. That order includes a real world in which the struggle between forces gives meaning to daily transformations, to history. It explains the here and now. The myth leads to the present, to the realities of the world and to human beings. The great cataclysms, even though they lead to an end—the necessary destruction of the world—are the bases of existence. It is a myth that is fulfilled by the earthly existence of humans. The fifth sun and humans were the corollary, the result of necessary antecedents. The *Anales de Cuauhtitlán* spoke about the existence of four kinds of beings before the true human species, about four kinds of food before maize. The myth created the dwelling, the time, and the resources of humans, as well as humans themselves.

There is a very important classifying element in the myths that I have not yet mentioned: color. The *Códice Vaticano Latino 3738* refers to the first four suns by the names Black Head, Yellow Head, Red Head, and White Head. These are the colors of the quadrants on the terrestrial plane. This reference leads to one about the installation of the four cosmic posts—the black post, the yellow, the red, and the white—at each of the corners of the world. They were supports for the sky and the pathways through which time flowed. Once they were erected, the only thing lacking was the counterclockwise movement that made the flow of time emerge from the east, the north, the west, and the south in cycles that would never cease while the world existed.

After the four prior cataclysms, and with the posts in place, where can we locate the initial spark that initiated the flow of time? It was the commission of the great sin: the union of the cold element with the hot element. The document called

Leyenda de los soles tells us that when the Sun of Water's deluge was over, the earth dried out and humans roasted the fish trapped in the mud when the water receded. The great sin was to roast the fish: it meant putting fire under cold, aquatic, dead matter. This began the alternation of time.

Today, in the highlands of Chiapas, they say that after the formation of the sun and the moon, there followed a time of silence during which the earth began to be populated.[2] Everyone, the gods and their creatures, was happy, but a very bad god called Antón Kristo came forth, adorned with three capes. The first cape was green, and it was filled with the torrential rains that cause floods. The second was red, the red of fire, and the third cape was white and carried sickness.

For centuries Antón Kristo used his capes against humanity, not allowing it a permanent existence. The other gods wanted to protect humanity, but Antón Kristo was so intelligent and powerful that he evaded them. The gods held a meeting, and Saint Thomas devised a plan. They would organize a feast with harps, guitars, and drums. They would dance and drink, and they would invite Antón. Indeed, Antón came, but he refused to stay because the time had come to end human life, and he had to produce a cataclysm. Then Holy Mary intervened. She began to dance with such rapid turns that her torn skirt gave a full view of her legs. Antón decided to stay, got drunk, and passed out.

Seeing him overcome, the gods undressed Antón and threw him on the road. Then they tried to destroy his capes. They burned two of them, but the water cape was not destroyed by the fire. When Antón Kristo recovered consciousness, he was indignant and complained about the gods' conduct. But he was

---

2 This story was taken from López Gómez, "La formación del cielo, del sol y la luna, y la maldición del Anticristo, el maíz."

disarmed. The gods captured him and tied him to the world's pillars.

Antón Kristo did not die. He is still bound to the posts. When he moves, he causes the earth to shake. Meanwhile, humans have multiplied and become separated, along with their gods, into the different groups of people. The great deluge has not yet arrived.

12

Tales about Opossums

In March 1985 I began investigating the myths that have as their hero a primitive Mexican mammal, the opossum. As is often the case when one becomes engrossed in a subject, month after month, my conversations grew obsessively focused on images of the marsupial and on beliefs and stories about it. This gave me a reputation as a "possumologist," and many of my friends began to contribute reports that helped a good deal in my study. Time went by, and I finished a book called *Myths of the Opossum,* but my friends continued to send me information. The material kept on accumulating like the piles of frog or owl figurines on collectors' furniture. At first I was sorry that some of the stories had not arrived in time to be included in the book, but later I encouraged my friends' contributions in the perhaps unrealistic hope of writing, at some undetermined time in the future, a study I could call something like *The Return of the Opossum.*

One of the tales I was sorry I had not heard sooner was told to me by a friend and colleague, Fernando Botas Vera. Fernando said that some thirty-four years ago, an old peasant from Tepexpan, whom everyone called don Chucho, warned him that it was dangerous to wander about the fields at night. Don Chucho said to Fernando, "The opossums go into the *arcinas* [*hacinas,* haystacks], and they live there. If you walk around the countryside at night, the thieves come out and rob you. If you pursue the thieves, you won't find them. What you will find are opos-sums. The opossums are the thieves' *naguales*."[1]

The story interested me, especially because the idea of opos-sum-*nagual* agrees entirely with a popular tale narrated in the Ojiteco language in 1945 by Raymundo Antonio from Santa Rosa in the Chinantla. The perceptive researcher Roberto J. Weitlaner picked up this story. It tells of the capture of an opos-sum thief who turned out to be the *nagual* of a young girl. Be-cause she was the animistic companion of the animal, she suffered the consequences of the punishment inflicted on it, and she complained about the lack of human understanding:

> They grabbed the opossum where he was stealing a chicken, and they burned the animal till only ashes were left. Because he was an opossum-*nagual*, her mother went the next day to recover the ashes in order to anoint her daughter with them, because the girl had awakened crying and saying, "They grabbed me, they burned me. Go bring the ashes. I was doing what I was supposed to, but the people envy me."[2]

Tales about the opossum-*nagual*, envisaged as the essence of thievery and incarnated in human bodies, would have supported one of the ideas I proposed in my book. In Mesoamerican reli-gion, supernatural forces were thought to be the essences that characterize the different beings in the human world. In my book, I used another account from the highlands of Chiapas as support for my proposal about *naguales*. According to the Tzotzil, the "opossum" force comes into the world as the dan-

---

1 Translators' note: Mesoamericans believed that people and gods could be transformed supernaturally into particular animals. *Nagual* refers both to the per-son so changed and to the alternate form. López Austin has proposed that this transformation was conceived as an infusion of particular supernatural forces or "essences." Some of these characterized *naguales*.

2 *Relatos, mitos, y leyendas de la Chinantla*, pp. 186–87.

gerous month *mol 'uch,* which dries up the crops if worshippers do not place on top of the entrances to their houses, all wrapped in maize leaves, offerings that include everything pleasing to the invisible marsupial—a small ear of corn, a small tortilla, a few beans, a cigarette, salt, and a little ball of *posol* (fermented maize dough).[3] The opossum force-essence, satisfied with the offering, will not attack the maize in the fields. In stories from Tepexpan and from Chinantla, the opossum-*nagual* that is not given an offering carries out his role by robbing travelers or killing chickens, which, together with maize and pulque, are his favorite food. That is why the girl companion of the opossum, instead of repenting of the theft, said, "I was doing what I was supposed to, but people envy me."

When the three stories are combined, they clearly fit together. Although they were told in places very distant from one another, they are linked, and like jigsaw puzzle pieces, together they acquire a significance that is hard to appreciate when they are separate. Why do these tales fit together? No doubt they come from old traditions, many of them now forgotten, that ended up as sayings, stories, myths, riddles, or beliefs. None of those popular expressions by itself can reveal the source of its meaning, but potentially each retains part of the message.

Now, as a collector, I continued to gather information about opossums whenever I could. In November 1990, while chatting with don Jesús Mazzo Nájar in Culiacan, I heard another interesting account. Don Jesús, who is famous for his knowledge of the folklore of Culiacan, told me that people there believe that on nights when there is a full moon, passers-by can suffer a real scare if they suddenly run into an opossum. The animal will abruptly rise before the person by coiling its tail as if it were a spring.

Don Jesús made it clear that for this apparition to take place, the night had to be one with a full moon. This is an important

3 Guiteras Holmes, *Los peligros del alma,* pp. 35–36, 281.

Figure 10. Zapotec vessel representing the Zapotec opossum god. It has ears of maize on its neck and a helix on its nose. From San Pedro Ixtlahuaca, Oaxaca.

component of the belief and not just a colorful addition. In the native tradition the opossum is part of a rich, meaningful complex. Pulque, the opossum's favorite drink, is one of its elements, as is the moon. We should remember that in the ancient Nahua religion, the moon goddess was also the goddess of pulque, and that the pulque deities wore the device called "moon nose jewel" under their noses.

The information about the lunar light was important, but what really surprised me was the way in which the opossum lifted itself up to frighten the traveler. I will explain why. The shape of the "spring" to which don Jesús alluded corresponds to the helix, an important Mesoamerican symbol. The helix was placed on the noses of opossums on ancient Zapotec ceramics (fig. 10), and centuries later it represented the noses of the gods of rain, as painted on numerous vessels deposited as offerings in the Templo Mayor of Mexico-Tenochtitlan. The helix represented the path the gods and their influences take. These influences composed time itself. In ancient times it was believed that divine forces, coming from the sky as well as from the underworld, arrived at the earth's surface gyrating along helical paths inside the trunks of the four sacred trees at the corners of the world. The gods who sat at those four cosmic extremes (in this particular case the *tlaloques,* or lords of rain) could exhibit on their own bodies the distinctive shape of the helix.

For his part, the opossum wore the helix because he was its creator. In the myths, the opossum not only stole fire and pulque but also created the cosmic path's helicoidal shape. For the Mazatec, the opossum was an old, drunken, wise man who, when consulted about the course a river should follow, advised that the current should make turns. This was an allusion to the helicoidal shape of the path time followed to reach the earth's surface.

The old opossum, the one who went to the other world to steal the possessions of the gods and bring them to the human world, had a great deal—too much—in common with the ancient god Quetzalcoatl, who was, among other things, the patron of thieves. The god himself was a thief. Quetzalcoatl stole the bones deposited in the World of the Dead and created humans from them, sprinkling the ground-up bones with blood from his penis. Afterward, he stole from Tonacatepetl maize kernels with which to feed humans. He also kidnapped the goddess Mayahuel in an adventure that ended with the creation of pulque, a drink that would bring happiness to his children. These were the thefts of maize and pulque, like those attributed to the good opossum.

There is more. Among the elements that correspond in Quetzalcoatl and the opossum there was, of course, the helix. At times, Quetzalcoatl's own body was twisted in an exaggerated

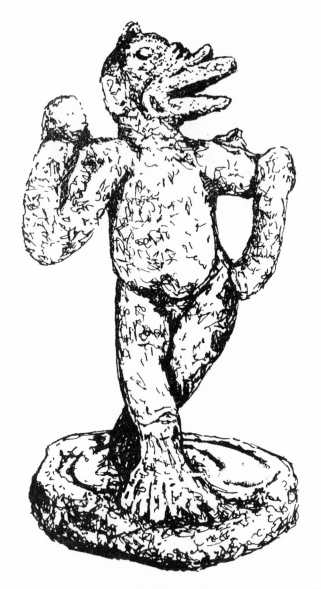

Figure 11. Monkey figurine with a Ehecatl-Quetzalcoatl (wind god) mask, found during construction of the metro system in Mexico City. It is standing on a coiled snake (National Museum of Anthropology, Mexico).

Figure 12. Preclassical clay whistle from Tlapacoya, Basin of Mexico (Arts and Sciences Museum, National University of Mexico, UNAM).

Figure 13. Andesite image of Ehecatl-Quetzalcoatl, possibly found in Castillo de Teayo, Veracruz (Rautenstrauch-Jöst Museum, Cologne).

Figure 14. The Mixtec Lord 9-Wind (Códice Vindobonensis *1964–1967:* pl. 5 *(xlviii).*

fashion resembling a rope. This can be seen in images of him and his avatars. A sixty-three-centimeter-high sculpture of a monkey was found during excavations for the metro in Mexico City; it is now in the National Museum of Anthropology (fig. 11). The monkey is twisted in an exaggerated form, and as if that symbolism were not enough, it stands on a coiled serpent. This animal, in its strange position, wears a distinctive mark on its face, the half-mask characteristic of the wind god Ehecatl-Quetzalcoatl.

Two other figures resemble each other to a remarkable degree, despite being separated by a striking length of time. The older one, which dates from the Preclassic period, is a whistle from Tlapacoya in which the body of a person with prominent lips (similar to the half-mask of the wind god) is a helix (fig. 12). The whistle's mouthpiece is a conical cap. The other is a stone sculpture representing Ehecatl-Quetzalcoatl, possibly found in Castillo de Teayo, Veracruz. It is now in the Rautenstrauch-Jöst Museum in Cologne. Like the whistle, its body is a helix, it has a conical hat, and its half-mask is a birdlike beak (fig. 13).

Another curious figure is that of the Mixtec Lord 9-Wind from the *Códice Vindobonensis* (fig. 14), shown as a bearded character with a rounded end to his loincloth, as is proper for Quetzalcoatl, and with his characteristic conical cap. His body is so twisted that he seems to have been changed into a rope.

The "spring" is thus explained. A millenarian tradition still provides a profound meaning for scattered, apparently arbitrary and unique, almost inadvertent symbols. Today, a popular belief that might be only a humorous warning to the traveler acquires other meanings when the light of past symbolism reveals its kinship with the great mystery of time's arrival in the world of humans.

13

The Name
Tarasca

Human groups often have two kinds of names: the one they give themselves and the ones other people use to designate them. The Diné, for example, are known by others as the Navajo ("Apaches from Navahu"), which is what their neighbors, the Tewa, called them. The Ñusabi, or "people of the clouds," were called Mixtecah (Mixtec) by the Nahua, who did not change the original meaning of the name but simply translated it into their language. The Hñahñu, or Ñäñho, were called Otontin (Otomi), a name also possibly derived from Nahuatl. The same was true for many other peoples.

The names given by outsiders may displease the recipients. The right for people to name themselves is clearly proper and reasonable. We should not be surprised, then, that there have been frequent protests by people insisting that they be called by the name they have chosen for themselves. This demand is sometimes hard to meet, especially when the imposed name has already diffused widely or when the change would pose problems in writing, pronunciation, or pluralization in the foreign languages that would be using it.

Viability and fairness do not always march to the same tune. Neither do the proper meaning of the name and the wish to keep it or to change it. Some groups willingly accept a name that contains an error or an incorrect meaning, whereas others are unhappy with a name that they incorrectly consider pejorative. An example of the former are the Gypsies. Gypsies were given that name because they were thought to be Egyptians—the same reason that in Hungary they were called Faraonemzetség, "the race of the Pharaoh." It is true that there were Gypsies in the north of Africa in the ninth century   , but they had come recently from the Taurus region after abandoning India, their original country, at some imprecisely known time. There is no relationship either ethnically or historically between Gypsies and Egyptians, but it pleases Gypsies to be considered Egyptians, and even more to be the descendants of pharaohs.

One name that has a complex semantic history and great variation in its acceptance is "Chicano," which originally applied to a Mexican who did not yet have many roots in the United States; it distinguished him from a *pocho,* who was more acculturated to American traditions. Subsequently, the name came to refer to the Chicano's economic situation, which was usually below that of the *pocho,* whose longer residence had allowed him to attain a higher economic level. The name Chicano, with this shade of meaning, was used contemptuously, at least in Texas. This limited and disparaging meaning, however, has been changed, through the efforts of many Americans of Mexican origin, to one with dignity and a deep political sense. Today the name is borne with pride.

Perhaps the names that satisfy human groups the most are those that stem from religious traditions. Some such names are historical, others mythical. Among peoples with historical names are the Druse, a mountain group who live in Syria, Lebanon, and Israel. Druse (*duruz*) is the plural of *darazi* (tailor), the name and trade of Ismael Darazi, the spiritual leader who guided the people in the eleventh century

Names that refer to a myth, a god, or a hero whose human-divine characteristics are not differentiated possess a dignity owing to their ancient time of origin and to their ties to a meaning which, like all of those that are based on the fundamental symbols of a tradition, retains in its mystery multiple possible understandings. Fortunately, there are many such names. Some of them have simple histories; others are based on very old, lengthy mythical episodes or are deeply entrenched in the people's culture. One can find them by looking at the great mythologies, among them the Greek.

Helene, for example, was not only the eponymous ancestor of the entire Hellenic race but also the father or grandfather (according to the version of the myth) of Dorus, Ionius, Aqueus, and Aeolus, who originated, respectively, the Dorians, the Ionians, the Acheans, and the Aeolians. The Ionians and Aeolians were called Greeks (*graikoi*) because they worshipped the Gray Goddess, or Old One. The Spartans, "sown men," were born from the teeth of a monstrous serpent slain by Cadmus, who sowed them by orders of Athena. And Europa, source of the name of the European continent, was the name of a beautiful girl desired by Zeus, father of the gods, who transformed himself into a docile, white bull and carried the victim of his lust on his back over the sea. After transforming himself into an eagle, he violated her in a small grove of willow trees after they arrived on the coast of Crete. The name Europa probably comes from "broad face," an epithet for the lunar goddess, and thus the whole episode seems to refer to a celestial process.[1]

Our Mexican traditions are also rich in mythical eponyms. Accounts of the ancient Nahua of the high Central Plateau name Tenuch, Ulmecatl, Xicalancatl, Otomitl, and Mixtecatl, the ancestors of the Tenochca, Olmec, Xicalanca, Otomi, and Mixtec peoples, as children of a celestial god and an earthly goddess. The following, among many others, are also eponymous ancestors: Cuextecatl (of the Cuexteca or the Huastec), Tlamatzincatl (of

---

[1] The relation of the name of the Greeks to the Gray or Old Goddess, and of Europa to the broad-faced lunar deity, has been discussed by Robert Graves in several of his books (*Greek Myths*).

the Tlamatzinca), Aculli (of the Aculhua), Chichimecatl (of the Chichimec), and Mazatl Tecuhtli (of the Mazatec).

The name Taras, a god mentioned in Bernardino de Sahagún's texts, should also be added to the list. Indeed, when the Franciscan asked Nahuas to identify the principal groups with whom they had relationships and to explain the origins of their names, they answered that among those groups were the Michhuaque, also called Cuaochpanme and Tarasca. The name Michhuaque comes from the Mexica's calling Tzintzuntzan, the principal city of the Tarascans, Michuacan (Place of Those Who Have Fish). Cuaochpanme (Those with a Broad Stripe on Their Heads) refers to the close haircut that some of these people used. Friar Bernardino explained the third name this way: "The god they had was called Taras; the Michhuaque, taking his name, were also called Tarasca. In the Mexican language this Taras god is called Mixcoatl, the god of the Chichimec."[2]

The term *Tarascan,* however, has been explained in less prestigious ways, which no doubt have contributed to making it less reputable. Nicolás León refers to their explanations.[3] The first explanation came from its similarity to the term *tarhascue,* which Friar Joan Baptista de Laguna said meant "my father-in-law, mother-in-law, son-in-law or daughter-in-law." Certainly there is a resemblance between the two words, but it is not apparent that *tarhascue* was the source of the name. To assert that it was, a reasonable chain of inference would have to be established between the term and the designation. Because there were no such good arguments—as is often the case—forced and trivial explanations were invented.

The first was put forth by Friar Joan Baptista. According to him, when the Spaniards reached Michoacan, the first person

2 Sahagún, *Historia general de las cosas de Nueva España,* vol. 2, book 10, chapter 29, paragraph 12, pp. 669–70.

3 León, "¿Cual era el nombre gentilicio de los tarascos y el origen de este último?"

they met was looking for her son-in-law. The Spaniards heard her and, not understanding the language, called the natives Tarasca. The second explanation, almost as trivial as the first, comes from the *Chronicles of Michoacán,* which tells about three Spaniards who went to trade goods with the *cazonci* [ruler] Tzintzicha:

> Before they left, the Spaniards asked the Cazonci for two Indian girls from among his relatives. And took them along, lying with them along the road. The Indians who traveled with them called the Spaniards *Tarascue,* which in their language means son-in-law. Later the Spaniards began to apply this name to the Indians, but instead of calling them *Tarascue,* they called them *Tarascos,* which is the name they have now, and the women are called *Tarascas.*[4]

The *Chronicles of Michoacán* not only gave this useless and preposterous explanation but also added that the natives were ashamed of it: "They are quite embarrassed by these names."

León gave another explanation that increased the pejorative tone of the term *Tarascan.* It concerned a supposedly historical episode in which the Mexica mocked the people whom they had not been able to defeat in battle. The story comes from Veytia and tells about the supposed joint migration of the Tarasca and the Mexica. The name turns out to be onomatopoeic.

> [The Teochichimec historians] say that all of them coming along together, some squadrons went ahead, and coming to a strait or a branch of the sea, which some people say was the Toluca river that empties into the sea of the south, along the western part in relation to New Spain, they decided to cross it by making rafts from tree trunks. Not having anything to tie the trunks together, they took off their maxtlis, which were cotton strips more than four braces long, and a span and a half wide, which they used to cover their

4 *Chronicles of Michoacán,* p. 69.

shameful parts, like a kind of truss, and this was the only clothing they wore. They tied the trunks together and made rafts to cross to the other side of the river with their wives and children. In doing this their maxtlis were torn and lost. Finding themselves completely naked, they asked the women to give them their shifts, which were short, without sleeves, came only to their thighs, and had an opening in the upper part for their heads to go through and two at the sides for their arms. Today they call this piece of clothing cotón, and it is much used by poor people. The men were able to cover themselves from their necks to their thighs, and the women had only their petticoats, and the upper part of their bodies were naked. Because the men had nothing to bind them from the waist down, their genital parts could be seen, and bounced on their thighs as they walked; and the women's breasts were bare, because they lacked undershirts or cotones. The squads who had remained behind, who they said were Mexica, Teochichimec and others, also crossed the strait on rafts but they were able to do so without getting rid of their clothes. When they overtook the advance party, seeing their nakedness and shame, they mocked them, and that was the reason they separated, the first ones remaining in the land of Michoacán. The Mexica called them Tarascas, because of the sound their genitals made on their thighs as they walked.[5]

After telling that malignant story, León evaluated the different versions of the name's origin. He didn't believe in a god called Taras because he did not find him cited sufficiently in the sources. Unjustifiably, in my opinion, he accepted the trivial account from the *Chronicles of Michoacán*. I believe he accepted this version because the name Tarasca was still rejected by the natives, who called themselves Purépecha. Taking into account that *purépecha* meant "commoner," he stated the reason for that self-designation: "Gilberti interprets the meaning of the word [*purépecha*]. We do not agree that this was the gentile [precon-

5 Veytia, *Historia antigua de México,* vol. 1, book 2, chapter 13, pp. 295–96.

quest] name of the people of Michoacán, and if contemporary people allow it and keep it, it is because the noble and lofty race is gone, and only the commoners and *macehuales* remain."[6]

The explanation León gave for the term *purépecha,* or *p'urhé-pecha,* does not convince me. It is more likely that, like the Nahuatl word *macehualli,* it refers in a narrow sense to commoners and in a broader sense to human beings. That would mean that the group called itself "the people," which is what usually happens. There are many groups who simply call themselves "humans" or "people." A sufficient example is *alemán,* "German." It meant "the totality of the people" or "all of humankind." Although the name Tarasca seems strange to some of the people whom it designates, it is possible that at least some of them had Taras as their patron god, that they got their name from him, and that the Mexica generalized excessively, as they did in using the toponym *Michoacan* to designate the entire territory ruled by the *cazonci.*

Previously, I stated a different view—that it was more plausible that the name came from a foreign language.[7] Now, however, I believe there is merit in Pedro Carrasco's argument that the words *thaRés* (images of the gods) and *thaRé* (old) are related.[8] It is probable that Taras, an old god related to fire (like Mixcoatl), was the patron god of a *p'urhépecha* people and produced a particular name that the Mexica generalized. In other words, there is no good reason to believe that *p'urhépecha* meant "commoner" in a strict sense or that Tarasca derived from "brother-in-law" or "son-in-law." Attributing a derogatory meaning to the second name is unjustified.

Today, Tarasca and *p'urhépecha* are acquiring different values. *P'urhépecha* has been reaffirmed as a prestigious name, one of pride in belonging to an ethnic group.

6 León, "¿Cual era el nombre?"

7 López Austin, *Tarascas y mexicas,* pp. 18–19.

8 Carrasco, "La importancia de las sobrevivencias prehispánicas en la religión tarasca: La lluvia," p. 271.

{14}
Our
First Parents

I am reading *History of the World in 10½ Chapters,* by Julian Barnes, and I think, half seriously and half in jest, about the endless possibilities for literary creation and re-creation beginning with a myth. The first chapter tells about the journey of the biblical ark from the viewpoint of a stowaway. You can be sure that the account is not favorable to the patriarch Noah! Barnes tells us the other story, the unofficial story.

Myths are like Tlalocan: they join apparent opposites. They unite what has always been old to what always retains its freshness. They are fertile fields for reinvention and reinterpretation. As sources, they offer adventures that are polished as they glide over roads traveled and traveled again in the past. Their narrations sum up wisdom's most exquisite ingredient, time itself. They go from one epoch to another, from one tradition to another, from one religion to another, acquiring new functions and supporting new paradigms. But at their core, in what could be called the heart of myths, they condense an extract of times and of history capable of fascinating almost forever. Myths are (almost) universal. They have become (almost) common denominators of the dissimilar histories of humanity.

Let us be cautious, however, about universals or archetypical dreams as sources of myths. Are myths from different parts of the world that much alike? Many claims of identity are based on fictitious similarities. Our own myths have made themselves at home in one of the favorite corners of our thought, there where cultural factors make us perceive the world in a way that we believe to be *the way*. Our myths become the grid by which we assimilate foreign myths, reducing their differences by the force of their similarities. There can be no doubt that astonishing similarities exist; myths do not represent thousand-year-old distillations in vain. But there are also amazing differences among myths, and those differences are based on rich historical peculiarities.

When Christians first confronted native myths, they saw agreements and disagreements with their own beliefs. The similarities posed a delicate question. Was there a vague memory among the natives of revelations made to an ancestral humanity? What kinds of preternatural inspirations had inspired the making of native myths? Christians wavered between attributing their invention to authentic primeval revelations, now almost forgotten, or to the deceit of the devil, who might have based his lies on the true revelations. Thus, among the Christians some held that "it is clear that the Devil told them one truth in order to make them believe a thousand lies."[1]

In spite of that warning about the falseness of the myths, the adventures of the gods continued to disturb the Christians because they saw too many parallels with biblical tradition. They couldn't stop comparing the two. Tamoanchan, for example, the place where the gods sinned by breaking the branches of the sacred tree, could be taken to be the earthly Paradise. Oxomoco and Cipactonal were pointed out as the native equivalent of Adam and Eve, and the trip Tata and Nene made during the flood at the time of the sun's demise was thought to be analogous to that of Noah and his family.

There are many examples of comparable myths, and the question of why there is similarity among myths from different cul-

1 *Historia de México*, p. 104.

tures still generates interesting debates. A lot of ink has been spilled over this topic, not only by scholars but also by those who want to find evidence of a single revealed truth everywhere. There is a wealth of material on the topic of similarities, but for the moment I want to deal with the peculiarities of the Meso-american tradition, and particularly with the characteristics of Oxomoco and Cipactonal, our first parents, according to ancient Nahua beliefs.

This is not a simple matter. First, accounts about Oxomoco and Cipactonal are brief and contradictory.[2] Second, the accounts are found in a heterogeneous ensemble of creation myths about the first humans, among which are the following:

1. Myths that refer to a first human couple, Oxomoco and Cipactonal.
2. Myths about the human generations that lived in each of the so-called suns.
3. The myth about the creation of the first man and woman during the fifth sun, from the bones obtained from Mictlan by Quetzalcoatl.
4. Myths about the men and women who were created to wage war to provide hearts and blood for the sun.
5. Myths about the creation of different human groups by their patron gods.

Here I will deal only with the first type of account.

The first contradiction in the sources referring to Oxomoco

2 Texts can be found in the following sources: *Historia de los mexicanos por sus pinturas* (pp. 25, 27, 33); *Códice Telleriano-Remensis* (part 2, pl. 22); *Anales de Cuauhtitlán* (pp. 3–4); *Leyenda de los soles* (p. 121); Mendieta, *Historia eclesiástica indiana* (vol. 1, p. 106); Sahagún, *Historia general de las cosas de Nueva España* (vol. 1, book 4, chapter 1, p. 235; vol. 2, book 10, chapter 29, paragraph 14, p. 672); Ruiz de Alarcón, *Tratado de las idolatrías* (pp. 39, 128, 130); and Fernández de Oviedo y Váldez, *Historia general y natural de las Indias* (vol. 11, part 3, book 4, chapter 2, p. 74).

and Cipactonal concerns their names. Sahagún and the *Códice Telleriano-Remensis* say that Oxomoco was the woman and Cipactonal the man, but the other sources say the opposite. Fernández de Oviedo y Valdés, referring to the Nicarao of Nicaragua, said that they called the original couple Tamagastad and Cipatonal. Cipactonal's name has a simple translation, "Sign of Cipactli," which links the character to the sign of the first day of the calendar, which belongs to the earth goddess. The translation of Oxomoco is more difficult. Ruiz de Alarcón proposed "Two Pine Torches Smeared with Turpentine Ointment," but that meaning, if correct, would be very hard to interpret.[3]

Do Oxomoco and Cipactonal resemble Adam and Eve? Adam and Eve were human. Although Eve has been identified with the Hurrian goddess Hawwa, the mother of every living thing, and with the Hittite goddess Hepatu, and although Jerusalem's guardian hero was said to be Adam's precursor, they were clearly human beings in the two biblical versions of the creation of humanity. The elderly Oxomoco and Cipactonal, on the other hand, appear in the sources sometimes as humans, sometimes as gods. They were credited with the birth of humanity, but it was also clearly stated that they belonged to "the company of the gods." The Nicarao said that Tamagastad and Cipatonal created the sky, the earth, the stars, the moon, humans, and everything else, and that they themselves were not created.

It was said that Oxomoco, because of a sin, had been converted into the goddess Itzpapalotl or "Obsidian Butterfly." This is interesting because Oxomoco and Cipactonal appear in the myths as characters who lived in the time of myth, at the time of the creation of the skies, the earth, and the underworld. They were created by Quetzalcoatl and Huitzilopochtli before the arrival of the fifth sun, when the half-sun that gave little light ruled over the sky. It was also said that they were the parents of the god

---

3 Ruiz de Alarcón, *Treatise on the Heathen Superstitions*, p. 232.

Piltzintecuhtli and therefore the grandparents of Cinteotl, the maize god.

Like Adam and Eve, as archetypes of the human race, Oxomoco and Cipactonal were associated with work. In the myth, the gods gave the elderly couple work. The woman was to spin, weave, and handle the maize kernels to cure and to foretell the future. Those arts certainly became feminine activities. The man—or both of them, because the source is not clear about it—was charged with cultivating the earth. This component is quite different in the biblical myth, in which work is a punishment imposed on humans as a consequence of an act involving the original pair. For the ancient Nahua, work was essential for humans because the gods had created Oxomoco and Cipactonal with an indisputable command: "Do not waste your time, but always labor."[4]

The results of such a mandate are noteworthy. In the Christian tradition, death liberates—it frees humans from work because work is something not essential but acquired as part of their history. Death sent humans either to a happy time of repose or to a useless time of suffering. Mesoamericans, however, believed that humans continued to work in the afterworld, wherever their destiny might lead them, because work was inherent in them.

Oxomoco and Cipactonal were archetypes of what is old, of wisdom, work, cultivating the earth, spinning, weaving, divining, and handling the calendar and therapeutic magic. But they were much more than that. Underlying the dual image of the two characters was a cosmic principle that generated the mythical attributes of the two old people. Was the nature of Adam and Eve similar? In Alexandria in the first century   , the philosopher Philo, in his attempt to logically connect Jewish theology and Greek speculation, attributed an allegorical nature to Adam and Eve. Adam represented reason, and Eve, sensuality. Regard-

4 *Historia de los mexicanos por sus pinturas,* p. 25.

Figure 15. Oxomoco as an old female diviner with maize kernels, and Cipactonal as an old priest (*Codex Borbonicus,* pl. 21).

less of whether or not Philo was correct, the difference between the first biblical parents and the first Nahua parents is fundamental. The attributes Philo gave to Adam and Eve did not transcend what is human, whereas Oxomoco and Cipactonal incarnated the generative bases of cosmic dynamics.

In effect, the division of the sexes and the constant reference to the calendar leads one to consider the Old Man and the Old Woman as activators of the alternation of the two forces—hot and cold—that constitute time. They are constantly linked to time-destiny and to the calendar. The sources name them as the inventors of the count of days and of the art of divination, as the ones who named the periods of time, and as the protectors of each of the "months," or twenties.

They are shown this way iconographically, face to face, with wrinkled skin and bristling hair, armed with an incense burner, a bone awl, and the priestly bag, noting the day signs or foretelling the future with knotted cords or with kernels of maize they throw on the ground. Their images are found in the *Codex Borbonicus* (fig. 15), in the *Códice Florentino* (fig. 16), and on a carved stone in Coatlan, Morelos (fig. 17). And they recently

Figure 16. Two old diviners using maize kernels and knotted cords (*Códice Florentino*, book 4, fol. 3v).

appeared during the excavation of the ceremonial site at Tlat-elolco, when a mural was discovered in the Calendar Temple, or Temple of the Glyphs, as reported by Salvador Guil'liem Arroyo (fig. 18).[5] The images seem to support Sahagún's and the *Códice Telleriano-Remensis*'s version of the names. In the *Codex Borbonicus* and on the Coatlan stone, the male is associated with the Cipactli sign. In Coatlan, the woman has a butterfly headdress. In Tlatelolco, the goddess Itzpapalotl's symbol, the "obsidian butterfly," seems to correspond to the woman.

Oxomoco and Cipactonal were personifications of the division and opposition of time's substance. But if they were a pair in opposition, how is it that in one account they appear not as a couple but as part of a group of four characters? Sahagún mentioned four old sages as the creators of the calendrical books: Oxomoco, Cipactonal, Tlaltetecuin, and Xochicahuaca.[6] Apart from Ruiz de Alarcón's incantations, in which the name Tlaltete-

5 Guil'liem Arroyo, "Descubrimiento de una pintura mural en Tlatelolco."

6 Sahagún, *Historia general de las cosas de Nueva España,* vol. 2, book 10, chapter 29, paragraph 4, p. 672. Tlaltecuin appears as Ixtlilton in vol. 1, book 1, chapter 16, pp. 178–79.

Figure 17. Oxomoco as an old woman also called Itzpapalotl, and Cipactonal as an old man writing the sign of the day on a stone in Coatlan, Morelos (Krickeberg 1969).

cuin is attributed to the earth, no other source mentions them. Could they be another pair of complementary opposites? Their names might make one think so. Xochicahuaca means "He Warbles with Flowers," or "Flowery Warble." Flower is the symbol of fire, of the aspect of time with a hot and celestial nature. Tlaltetecuin means "One Who Makes the Earth Resound," or "He Who Strikes the Earth." Where in that name is there a reference to the cold, aquatic element? The answer lies in the rituals to petition for rain addressed to the cold underground world. María Elena Aramoni, describing contemporary Nahua traditions in the Sierra Norte de Puebla, says that the way water is requested from the underworld gods is to beat on the ground to make sure that they hear.[7] The rattle-sticks of the ancient Nahua priests were a similar type of petition. Both characters, Xochicahuaca and Tlaltecuin, were identified by their sound. Xochicahuaca's was fiery, Tlaltetecuin's, aquatic. When reading Sahagún's text,

7 Aramoni Burguete, *Talokan Tata, Talokan Nana: Hierofanías y testimonios de un mundo indígena*, pp. 178–79.

Figure 18. The two old people. Detail of a mural from the "Calendar Temple" in the ceremonial precinct of Tlatelolco.

one should think not about a group of four old men but about a group composed of two oppositional pairs.

Did Adam and Eve resemble Oxomoco and Cipactonal? Yes, inasmuch as in both traditions the origin of humankind was attributed to a first couple. They are similar only in what is obvious.

{15}

The Left Hand,
the Right Hand

What resemblance more perfect than that between our two hands! And yet what a striking inequality there is!

To the right hand go the honors, flattering designations, prerogatives: it acts, it orders, and *takes*. The left hand, on the contrary, is despised and reduced to the role of humble auxiliary: by itself it can do nothing; it helps, it supports, it *holds*.

The right hand is the symbol and model of all aristocracies, the left hand of all plebeians.

What are the titles of nobility of the right hand? And whence comes the servitude of the left?[1]

Those are the words at the beginning of an essay that E. E. Evans-Pritchard considered to be one of the best ever written in the history of sociology. It was a brief piece, now a classic, written by Robert Hertz, a young student in a group assembled by Émile Durkheim in connection with the *Année Sociologique*. Hertz was destined to be one of the outstanding sociologists of his time, but his brilliant career was cut short by the First World War. On April 13, 1915, a few months after publishing this famous essay, the young sociologist was killed by a German machine gun during the attack on Marchéville.

The essay was published as "La préeminence de la main droite: étude sur la polarité religieuse." It dealt with symbolic classification. As Evans-Pritchard noted, the essay drew conclusions that today seem obvious, but they are obvious because Hertz made them so. He showed that among very different peoples of the

---

1 Hertz, "The Pre-eminence of the Right Hand: A Study in Religious Polarity."

world, the cultural differentiation between the hands was one of the most notable manifestations of a total taxonomic division.

Dualism, which Hertz found to be essential in so-called primitive thought, dominated social organization. According to him, this domination caused primitive people to divide the universe into halves that were, in religious terms, opposed and complementary. The community was not the only thing that was divided in two: all of the universe was carved into halves in which beings and forces attracted or repelled each other according to their location. Hertz, analyzing the ideas of the groups he studied, said that in this total taxonomic division, on one side lay strength, good life, the sky, maleness, light, day, east, and south; on the other side were weakness, evil, death, earth, femaleness, darkness, night, north, and west. He added that the human body also fell under this universal classification, and that the physiological advantages of the right hand made sense according to oppositional ideas that already existed in the collective consciousness. In religious terms, then, the right hand became sacred, the left hand, profane.

In 1973, Rodney Needham published a book, *Right and Left: Essays on Dual Symbolic Classification,* honoring Hertz. The book, justly, tried to highlight a work that was less well-known than it deserved to be. As is often the case in science, Hertz's work did not produce immediate results. It was not until 1933 that articles began to appear about the symbolic value of the right and left hands in the different cultures of the world, among them peoples in China, Africa, and the central Celebes. Those studies were inspired, directly or indirectly, by Hertz's essay. Needham's book contains several of those articles, as well as more recent ones.

Today, research on dualism, which Hertz inspired, is one of the most interesting areas in anthropology. Taxonomic duality has been studied primarily, but not exclusively, by the structuralists. They have shown that there existed in ancient societies a general, or almost general, dualistic principle for classifying the universe. The omnipresence of the partitioning principle has kept the question of its origin alive. That is, does the classification of everything in the world into two sets arise from innate characteristics of humans, or is it a cultural product, present since antiquity, whose nature is revealed in the particular classificatory features of each culture?

Most studies have shown that despite similarities in the ways people divide the cosmos, and despite disconcerting coincidences, each culture constructs its own intricate classifications based on unique principles. They differ in degree of complexity; in China, for example, dualism created an impressive philosophical composite based on the great opposition of yin and yang. They differ in content, as in the case of Egypt, where, contrary to the case in most other parts of the world, the earth was male and the sky female. They differ in their mechanisms of classification, which sometimes cause interesting inversions owing to their systems of oppositions and homologies.

There is an interesting example of that kind of inversion in the Mediterranean. A house is pictured as an inverted microcosm. Pierre Bourdieu studied the dwellings of the Bedouins of the Maghreb and discovered a set of symbolic values in the internal and external orientation of the house with regard to the position of the sun. As a rule, the house of a Bedouin faces east, so that the sun's rays light up the back wall, the exterior of which faces west. The eastern wall of the house is dark inside. This illumination results in a 180-degree change in the cardinal points inside the house. The illuminated inner wall was "the one plastered by men's trowels," while the eastern wall was "whitened and hand-decorated by women."

Like all traditional classifications, this one's use was not limited to the locations of beings in the cosmos but was also applied to governing daily actions. The functions, activities, and distribution of people, animals, and things inside a house were based on an inversion that obeyed the interior order. Thus, sick people were laid down against the dark wall; the northern interior was the animals' space, and the south was for humans. The wall to the right as a person entered the house was the place allocated to food stores, but grain for sowing was kept in the dark part. All of inner space acquired a meaning based on the opposition of light and dark, night and day, low and high, feminine and masculine.[2]

Dual classification was very important for Mexican natives. Mesoamerican studies of binary oppositions gained importance beginning with the study of the duality of the Supreme God. Belief in a Supreme God, conceived to be the fusion of all the gods, was present in the different Mesoamerican cultures. Among the Maya it was Hunab Ku, among the Zapotec, Pijetao, and among the Nahua, Tloque Nahuaque. Their dual nature was expressed in some of their names, either through a single name (for example, Ometeotl, "Dual God"), or through two names, one given to each of the complementary components (for example, the feminine Omecihuatl, "Dual Lady," and the masculine Ometecuhtli, "Dual Lord").

In recent years the studies have diversified and proliferated. One of the results was the recent book *Mesoamerican Dualism,* consisting of presentations made at the Forty-sixth International Congress of Americanists.[3] There have also been notable ethnographic studies of dualism, many of them owing to William Madsen's investigations of contemporary Nahuas in the southern part of the Valley of Mexico.[4]

One of the achievements of that kind of study was evidence of the role played by the daily lives of people in the formation of religious thought. It weakened the elitist concept that cosmovi-

2 Bourdieu, *An Outline of a Theory of Practice*, pp. 90-91.

3 Van Zantwijk, de Ridder, and Braakhuis, *Mesoamerican Dualism\Dualismo mesoamericano.*

4 Madsen, "Hot and Cold in the Universe of San Francisco Tecospa, Valley of Mexico"; *The Virgin's Children: Life in an Aztec Village Today.*

sion arose from the intellectual effort of aristocratic sages, and it favored the notion of an orderly perception of the world based on work and ordinary life. The dual division, instead of being produced by speculations, was the result of the order produced by daily existence.

Because of this, investigations of domestic space are particularly interesting. Although it is difficult to discover such arrangements in the remote past, archaeologists have indeed found significant evidence of prehistoric symbolism. In San José Magote, a Oaxaca town in the Etla Valley that flourished in the Early and Middle Preclassic periods (1700 to 500), archaeologists could delineate, because of the placing of utensils in the houses, separate domestic zones, some employed in feminine activities and others given to masculine work. Metates (grinding stones) and jars were to the right of the entrance, while flint chips and pieces produced by the masculine work of making scrapers, knives, burins, and drills were found on the left side.[5]

In a much more accurate way, ethnographers have recorded the meanings of domestic divisions among contemporary native peoples. One of the best works is Rosanna Lok's on the partition of the house among people of the Nahua town of San Miguel Tzinacapan, in the northern sierra of Puebla. She found an interesting projection of the cosmos centered on the comal, or griddle, on which tortillas are cooked. The comal functions as the surface of the earth, a plane that divides all of the universe into two parts. The process of producing food is charged with meanings that relate it to the sun's passing over the sky and through the underworld.[6]

Among the principal oppositional pairs in the Mesoamerican religious tradition were female/male, earth/sky, cold/hot,

5 Whitecotton, *The Zapotec: Princes, Priests, and Peasants,* p. 32.
6 Lok, "The House as Microcosm: Some Cosmic Representations in a Mexican Indian Village."

moon/sun, water/fire, dark/light, east/west, north/south (and the double opposition of west-east/north-south), lesser/greater, and rainy season/dry season. The opposition upon which Hertz based his studies—the difference between the two hands—is less common. It exists merely as an indication of the two halves of the earth's surface. It is found, as such, among the ancient Tarasca. The story said that Taríacuri consolidated his conquests, dividing the conquered territory in half in order to split the government among his Chichimec captains and his island allies. His people were given the "right hand," and his allies were given the left, which in that case corresponded to the "hot lands."[7]

There are, however, at least some comments that might indicate a polar division with respect to the control of the earth. One of these clues seems to link a "left part" of the world to the feminine supernatural domain. In a text from the Sierra Norte de Puebla describing a cure for *susto* (fright), doña Rufina Manzano, the curer, mentions the Virgin of Carmen. The sacred feminine figure is linked to the part of the cosmos that belongs to the left side. Doña Rufina literally referred to "the Holy Virgin of Carmen, who is said to rule the left side of the world."[8]

---

7 *Relación de las ceremonias . . . de Michoacán,* part 2, chapter 31, p. 153.
8 Segre, *Metamorfosis de lo sagrado y de lo profano,* p. 227.

{16}
Complements
and Compositions

An important sixteenth-century Nahuatl document, *Primeros memoriales,* or *Memoriales de Tepepulco,* begins its section on the food and drink of nobles with these words:

Tortillas folded in the middle, their complement is a dish of chilepiquín.

Tortillas stretched by handling, their complement is a dish of miltomate.

Tamales [in the shape of] "wrapped heads,"[1] their complement is a dish of pressed [chile] . . .[2]

The opposite page begins with a section on the food of commoners:

Tortilla crumbs.

Not [very] clean tortillas, their complement is tomato stew.

Tortillas made from strips of scraped heart of agave, their complement is chilmole.

Tortillas made of chaff, their complement is brine . . .[3]

---

1 This could refer to tamales with wrappings shaped like turbans or tangled hair.
2 Sahagún, *Primeros memoriales,* fol. 54v.
3 Sahagún, *Primeros memoriales,* fol. 55r.

The word *inamic,* translated here as "their complement," is used in other texts to describe medicines.[4] The medicines are the "complements" of the illnesses. In much the same way, a woman is the *inamic* of her mate, a warrior is the *inamic* of his enemy, a man becomes the *inamic* of his comrade, and a player is the *inamic* of his opponent in the game. Everything in the world has its complement, its opposite, its correspondent.

Today, as in the past, the idea of the complement exists. The Nahua of San Francisco Tecospa, in the federal district, certainly acknowledge the universality of complements.[5]

In the millenarian Mesoamerican tradition, the interaction of opposites produced a continuous maladjustment, a constant transformation in the world. If an element acquired too much energy, humans had to intervene and put contrary elements in place in order to maintain the balance that was necessary for their existence. If cosmic forces were left to operate freely, they could lead to chaos, either through the predominance of one or through the absolute equilibrium of the opponents, that is, through the destruction of opposites or the loss of the advantages produced by the transformations.

This balance of opposites was needed in every area of life. The Mocho give us a clear example of how such a balance is effected in native cultures today. Mocho tastes in matters of food are altered, according to Perla Petrich, by material factors (the abundance or scarcity of food), by physiological factors (the daily loss of energy), and by cultural factors (a particular concept of the body and the digestive process that endows certain foods with specific qualities, among them "cold" or "hot"). The Mocho envision the digestive process as composed of several stages, among them the "filtering" of the food. The filtering is done in the "cluster," a group of organs including the liver, the lungs, and

4 *Códice Florentino,* book 10, chapter 28, fol. 97r.
5 Madsen, "Hot and Cold in the Universe of San Francisco Tecospa."

the heart. The Mocho are convinced that in order to avoid trouble during filtration and to obtain proper nourishment, strict adherence to a complex gustatory code is necessary in the preparation and combination of foods.[6]

The need to follow a strict standard in eating food is more than the search for a calm digestion and an adequate diet. The rules preserve health and prevent the illnesses caused by disequilibrium. The diet should balance "cold" food and "hot" food. The force of the more or less permanent state of the human body, considered to be either "cold" or "hot," has to be ameliorated by food of the opposite nature. Cold illnesses should be treated with hot medicines, and vice versa. Just remember all the taboos that exist for menstruating women. There is still a firm belief that during her period (the loss of blood chills the body), a woman should avoid any food of a cold nature, including watermelons and lemons.

People have, and used to have, these sorts of prohibitions for pregnant women, new mothers, children, and the elderly. The ancient Nahua recommended that old people drink pulque because that "cold" drink moderated the heat that had accumulated in their bodies with the passage of time.

All of this demonstrates the predominantly practical nature of the classifications. Cosmovision was the result of the order that emerged through the centuries from the daily work of people and their relationships with nature, with their own bodies, and with their fellow beings. It was the search for harmony that believers considered necessary for their existence. Cosmovision, which was an abstraction and a systematizing of daily practices, fed back the practices as a guide to behavior and constituted a holistic explanation. In that way a flux and reflux of knowledge took place.

Classifications based on a simple dual opposition became

6 Petrich, *La alimentación mochó: Acto y palabra*, pp. 108, 131–34.

more complex with the addition of numerical or geometrical patterns or of combinations in which the quantitative and the qualitative were reciprocally derived. Speaking of the Tzotzil of Zinacantan, Evan Vogt says:

> Each plant is classified not only as wild or domesticated, or from the high country or the hot country, but also as to whether it has an innate soul, which is defined as being "hot or cold," "active or passive." Moreover, each soul has a color which, not surprisingly, came from the five basic Zinacantecan colors, red, black, white, yellow, and blue-green. As a rule, the soul's innate color did not correspond to the natural color of the flowers, leaves, or thorns.
> . . . Those five colors were generally the most salient in all of the Mayan cultures, and they were often associated with directions: red with the east, black with the west, white with the north, yellow with the south, and blue-green with the "center of the world."[7]

Obviously, the classification was intended to be based on the nature of the living things. Nature obeys the characteristics of the innate soul that resides inside it. The origins of the innate soul go back to the very birth of the world, to the time of myth, when the gods gave, with their own essence, an inner nature to creation. And the gods' essence, the "load," was composed of two elemental forces, designated as oppositional pairs—cold/hot, rainy season/dry season, rain/sun, feminine/masculine, lower/ upper, water/fire, death/life, dark/luminous—which, by their different proportions, made each class of beings distinct.

We must, therefore, keep in mind the two fundamental principles of Mesoamerican religion. First, every created thing can be classified into one or the other of the two great taxonomic divisions of the universe. Second, this classification derives from

7 Vogt, *Ofrendas para los dioses: Análisis simbólico de rituales zinacantecos,* pp. 18–19.

the predominance of one kind of force over the other. From the second principle originated the idea, like that in Chinese cosmovision, that nothing is a single pure being, composed solely of a fiery force of nature or solely of a watery one, but everything is formed from a combination of the two.

Thus, in principle, there are two great divisions whose essences are governed by opposing gods. Let us examine the case of plants in the thinking of the Sierra Totonac. According to them, at the time of the creation the division of plants was due to the intervention of two gods. The sun, with his blood and his warmth, created everything that blooms and grows above ground, including the chiles and the fruits. The opposing water god, Aktsini', today identified with Saint John the Baptist, created everything that grows and prospers underground, thanks to rain, particularly the tubers.[8]

As to the second principle, let us compare the Chinese symbol that represents the union of yin and yang—a circle formed by two equal, united parts, one black and the other white, each including a small circle of the other color to indicate that no being is entirely positive or negative. In the Mesoamerican tradition, the principle can be illustrated by the way in which symbols, as they divide, retain in each portion new possibilities for division. Examples of this are some of the symbols associated with the migration of the Mexica and their settling on the islands of Lake Texcoco. Many symbolic interactions appear in the sources. I will give only three of them.

The first refers to the Mexica during their migration. Considered, in the political context of that time, to be in the aggregate a solar people, they became divided into two groups. According to legend, the division took place before the founding of their two island capitals, when they passed through Cohuatlicamac. There, two bundles miraculously appeared. In one of them, the Mexica

8 Ichon, *La religión de los totonacas de la sierra,* p. 126.

found a beautiful, rich chalchihuite, or turquoise, and in the other, two sticks. The two groups quarreled over possession of the precious stone, but Huitziton, the leader of the group that later would be the Tenochca Mexica, convinced his people to let the Tlatelolca Mexica keep it, because the two sticks were tools used to make fire and were therefore the more valuable of the two.[9]

That remote, legendary event explains the division that took place at the time of the island settlements. A certain regularity appears in the symbolic values of north and south, the former aquatic, the latter fiery. The group with the fire founded Mexico-Tenochtitlan, the southern city; the group with the chalchihuite (symbolizing water) founded Mexico-Tlatelolco, the northern city. This was the same spatial arrangement as that of the halves of the main pyramid of Mexico-Tenochtitlan, the so-called Coatepec, the heart of the main temple. There were two chapels at its top. The northern one belonged to Tlaloc, the god of rain. The southern one belonged to Huitzilopochtli, the solar god of war.[10]

The second example pertains not to all of the Mexica but only to the group associated with fire, the Tenochca. Recall the miracle and the emblem of the city of Mexico-Tenochtitlan, which I described in chapter 9. The union of the eagle with the cactus made up an opposition in which the bird, corresponding to the name of Mexico, was the solar element, while the cactus and the stone, corresponding to the name of Tenochtitlan, were the aquatic element.

The solar element can be further analyzed as a third example. It was, in its turn, composed of two elements: the bird, which

9 Torquemada, *Monarquía indiana,* vol. 1, book 2, chapter 2, pp. 79–80.
10 This was how López Luján (*The Offerings of the Templo Mayor of Tenochtitlan,* pp. 294–96) explained the symbolism of the legend of the chalchihuite and the two sticks, the location of the two cities, and the orientation of the chapels of Tlaloc and Huitzilopochtli atop the pyramid.

Figure 19. Left: the sun god carrying the sun on his back. It has alternating angular symbols of lightning rays (fire symbols) and strips with chalchihuites (green beads), or water symbols (*Códice Telleriano-Remensis,* pl. 10). *Right:* the rain god carrying a lightning ray in his hand (*Códice Vaticano Latino 3738,* pl. 28).

was solar, and the serpent, which was aquatic. Every symbolic element, when it split off from a larger element, retained within it a new duality. Such characteristics were not unexpected in earthly beings because, in Mesoamerican religion, the gods themselves had complex essences. The complexity of the "loads" or "souls" of earthly beings was only a reflection of the nature of the gods. This point can be illustrated by looking at two gods with extreme characteristics: the sun god and Tlaloc, the first very fiery, the second strongly aquatic. The iconography is clear (fig. 19). In it, the solar disk has in each of its fiery, masculine rays a strip ending with a chalchihuite, the symbol of water. Tlaloc, the god of rain, is represented by two emblems of his attributes. In one hand he carries the vessel from which he pours water over the surface of the earth, and in the other, the fiery symbol of lightning.

Lightning makes the fiery nature of the rain god obvious. The aquatic nature of the sun needs to be explained. The sun sent daily to the earth's surface the irradiations of time, of destiny. Again we encounter complexity. Some forces of destiny were celestial; others issued from the underworld. Destiny was the composite of the gods, the gods above and the gods below—that is, the fiery gods and the aquatic gods.

17

Synonymies

The work of a scholar sometimes resembles that of a detective, not only in formulating a hypothesis and looking for adequate proof of it but also in devising a complete plan for investigation, including the methods and techniques needed for that particular case. Criticism is valuable during this creative process, particularly if it is pertinent and informed. If it comes from someone who holds an opposite opinion, it becomes a challenge, a spur to one's wits, and may resemble a game in which one move follows another in response to the competitor's tactics.

The topic of dualism through opposition of contraries gave rise to an interesting and productive debate on a specific problem in the Mesoamerican religious tradition: the cold/hot classification of food, health, disease, and medicine. Almost everyone is familiar, to some degree, with those topics. For example, there is the question of whether it is good or bad to eat certain kinds of food under particular circumstances because of their "cold" or "hot" nature. This is not a thermal classification. It has to do with the "quality" of the food, not its temperature. In this kind of classification, hail would be labeled "hot," while some recently cooked meat might be "cold."

The problem began to emerge in ethnography during the thirties. In Mexico, and among people of Mexican origin living in the southern part of the United States, researchers found a taxonomy based on these classificatory elements. Soon, similar ideas were discovered ethnographically in Guatemala, Colombia, Peru, and Chile. The accumulation of information brought the problem to a head. What was the origin of this dualism? Was it American or European?

During several decades, many of us participated in the debate. A key defender of a European origin was George M. Foster. According to him, the cold/hot classification in native American medicine came from the Hippocratic doctrine of humors. Hippocrates (c. 460–c. 370) based his doctrine on four elements sharing four primary qualities. Earth was dry and cold; fire was dry and hot; air was wet and hot; and water was cold and wet. Hippocrates said that the human body contained four liquids, or humors: blood, which corresponded to air; phlegm, which corresponded to water; yellow bile, which corresponded to fire; and black bile, or melancholia, which corresponded to earth. Equilibrium of the four bodily elements was necessary to maintain health.

Much later, Galen of Pergamum (second century) systematized medical thought, arguing that an excess of blood was the cause of plethora, an excess of phlegm the cause of dropsy, an excess of pituitary fluid the cause of colds and phlegmatic diseases, and an excess of bile the cause of indigestion—the last by clogging the digestive system and gastrointestinal tract with mucus.

Following Galen's ideas, Western medical thought concentrated for centuries on maintaining the body's humoral equilibrium. Medicines were classified as wet, dry, hot, and cold, and doctors prescribed them in attempts to modify the conditions of patients in accordance with their personal characteristics, the influence of the stars, environmental conditions, and the particular illness afflicting the person.

Foster argued that when Spanish medicine came to the New World, it degenerated from being a scientific pursuit. It became a native folk medicine by a process during which the qualities of dry and wet were lost and only those of hot and cold were retained.

Several of us opposed Foster. We believed that the polar opposition of cold and hot belonged to Mesoamerican thought as one of the expressions of the dual classification of the cosmos. Among many other reasons, we proposed that such a system extended beyond Mesoamerica, that it was widely diffused across the New World, and that it existed from very ancient times. We denied the possibility that a quaternary system could have deteriorated so automatically, uniformly, and rapidly over such a vast territory. We showed that some native names for both diseases and medicines had lexical elements that referred to the cold/hot system, and that native classifications often disagreed with Spanish classifications in both their attribution of qualities and their classificatory principles.

Bernard Ortiz de Montellano studied the classifications that Francisco Hernández, Philip II's *protomedico,* made of native medicines. He found that the Spanish doctor, in classifying the medicinal plants used in New Spain as hot or cold, not only diverged from native classifications but also, on several occasions, complained that in his judgment the native classification was baseless. The simple explanation is that the native classification was not based on the same principles as the Hippocratic one. Aside from the fact that both were based on a cold/hot opposition, they belonged to different systems. Francisco Hernández was unable to perceive this.[1]

One of the most convincing arguments used by those of us who maintained that the native opposition of cold and hot came from ancient Mesoamerican concepts was that in today's beliefs the dichotomy extends not just to health and disease but to all of

---

1 See a development of the argument in Ortiz de Montellano's excellent book, *Aztec Medicine, Health, and Nutrition,* pp. 27–28, 217.

the universe. The native system classifies not only plants, animals, minerals, and persons but also times, astral bodies, supernatural beings, meteors, processes, and so forth. That was the ancient Mesoamerican concept, and it differed from the Hippocratic system.

A debate solely about the degeneration of the Hippocratic system in America now seems pointless. Independently of the arguments presented by one side or the other, further investigations have clearly demonstrated two things. First, the pair cold/hot is only one of many that existed, and still exist, in the Mesoamerican religious tradition, together with underworld/sky, feminine/masculine, dark/light, rainy season/dry season, and many more that divide the universe into two parts. Second, many recent studies unrelated to the topics of health, illness, nourishment, or medicine show the Mesoamerican taxonomic system clearly. Today, Evans-Pritchard's opinion would be quite applicable to the Mesoamerican case: "In every language I know . . . certain qualities, moral and spiritual, are associated with the opposites of hot and cold."[2] Medicine and food were only a part of an immense complex, and they should be evaluated that way.

I do not intend to continue the debate at this time, but instead want to refer to one of the many methodological and technical results that have come from it: the discovery of a kind of synonymy through which the categories of the divisions can be interchanged with relative ease. One of Foster's strongest arguments was that we who defended the Mesoamerican origin of the cold/hot dichotomy did so on the basis of texts that were written phonetically in Latin script, that is, during the colonial era, and that therefore the native informants might have been influenced by Spanish thought. In order to refute that argument it was necessary to look for cases in which the opposition was expressed in terms other than cold/hot.

2 Evans-Pritchard, "Foreword," p. x, in Needham, *Right and Left.*

tlanatonavistli

Figure 20. Pictograph of "aquatic fever" (*tlanatonahuiztli*), caused by tooth disease (*Códice Florentino*, book 10, chapter 28, fol. 102r).

If Foster's thesis were true, we would find only hot/cold as an oppositional pair in the taxonomic system. On the other hand, if the division hot/cold were merely one of many expressions in a much larger and more complex system, the division would be expressed in many other ways, all of them equivalent and agreeing with the larger system. That plurality can be proved. It can be seen in the vast systems of opposites:

1. Synonyms of some of the elements of the pair cold/hot.
2. Synonymous pairs of cold/hot.
3. Substitution for the elements of some pairs by others, while the value of opposition is maintained.

Let us look at an example of the first kind of synonymy. Because of Foster's objection, a vigorous search for synonymies was undertaken. It was expected that, given the meaning of "cold" in native cosmovision, categories such as "water," "night," or "wind" might have been substituted for it because all of the aquatic, nocturnal, and windy elements correspond to the underworld. The cold diseases came from the underworld, from the region of the dead, from the region of the gods of rain, from the insides of hills. Indeed, an example of a synonym for "cold" appeared in a written text from the early colonial period, as well as in its pictographic representation. The logic of transference could not have developed in such a short time; this congruence came from a system different from the European one. We have already seen that "cold" is a quality, not a temperature. In Mesoamerican thought it was impossible for cold diseases to cause fevers. An example is the case of *tlanatonahuiztli* fever, caused by dental disease. The name of the ailment literally means "aquatic fever of the teeth," and it was depicted in the *Códice Florentino* by an image of teeth from which flowed a stream of water (fig. 20).[3]

In the second type of synonymy, diseases could be either cold or hot, depending upon whether they came from the underworld or the sky. The paths they came by were the same as the paths of destiny. They traveled through the four cosmic trees that held up the sky and sank their roots into the underworld at the corners of the world. Both good and evil circulated through the trunk and could be designated with different oppositional pairs. One of those pairs appears as a metaphor that refers particularly to diseases. Tropes formed by two complementary terms were common in the ancient Nahuatl language. Thus, the trope "night, wind" signified the undetectable character of the divinities; "the stick, the stone" signified punishment; "the juniper, the ceiba (silk-cotton tree)" signified authority and protection; "the earth, the mud" signified the human body; and there were many more.

In order to say "illness" in the abstract sense, there was an elegant Nahuatl metaphorical expression, "*in ehecatl, in temoxtli.*" Literally, it meant "the wind, the descent." The first term is clear: the winds, the "bad airs"—the forces that rise from the world of

3 *Códice Florentino,* book 10, chapter 28, fol. 102r.

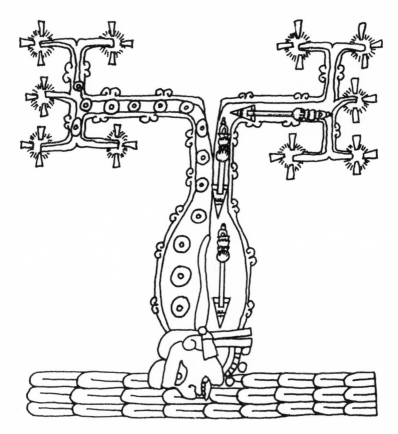

Figure 21. The cosmic tree, split in two, with chalchihuite symbols on the left and descending arrows on the right (*Códice Vindobonensis,* pl. xvi, p. 37).

the dead, harmful, cold entities and penetrate people's bodies to make them sick—were intimately associated with illness.[4] In the *Códice Vaticano Latino 3738,* this can be seen in the relationship between the god Nahui Ehecatl (4-Wind) and diseases.

They believed that Nahui Ehecatl was the god of the four winds, and that is actually what the name meant. The merchants held a

4 Concerning the prehispanic origin of these beliefs, see López Austin, "El mal aire en el México prehispánico."

great feast for him, but when the fifth day began, they did not dance or dare to leave their houses, because they thought that the illness that was fated for that day was so dangerous that no one could escape it, and so, even when they were traveling on the road on that day, they came to a halt.[5]

The second term of the metaphor, "descent," is simply a direct reference to the hot illnesses, because they came from the upper part of the cosmos. They were the diseases that came down from the sky. The two terms, "descent" and "wind," make sense reciprocally.

López Luján, identifying the element "descent" with the image of a descending arrow, found the opposition in the halves of a cosmic cruciform tree depicted in the *Códice Vindobonensis* (fig. 21).[6] Like many other portrayals of cosmic trees, it is divided, and it is characterized by differentiating elements. In the right half are the descending arrows; on the left are the chalchihuites, the perforated green precious stones that are one of the most important symbols of water.

From "the wind, the descent," one can go on to the third kind of synonymy. An ancient metaphor, recorded by Rémi Siméon in his *Dictionary*,[7] can be found nowadays in a different native language, keeping one of its elements but changing the other one for an equivalent that still fits within the system. In the Mazatec ceremony called *wincha,* the "man of knowledge" intones a prayer in which he asks that no enemies who cause illnesses be allowed to exist, and he refers to them by saying, "And let there be no one who talks to the wind, to the light [to cause harm]."[8] In another part of the same ceremony he again prays:

---

5 *Códice Vaticano Latino 3738,* pl. 27, p. 70.
6 López Luján, *The Offerings of the Templo Mayor of Tenochtitlan,* p. 298.
7 Siméon, *Diccionario de la lengua náhuatl o mexicana.* See *temoxtli,* p. 472.
8 Boege, *Los mazatecos ante la nación,* p. 142.

For the good of our home, of our family, of our children, let the
evils not enter my house, my home; let the evils that are made
with light, with the winds, the diseases and all the bad things there
are, let them not touch my children, my family.[9]

Now the hot evils, those coming from the sky, are characterized by another of the images that refer to their nature as being
light, which makes them celestial beings, in opposition to the
winds, which come from the place of darkness. One of the elements in the metaphor has changed, but the meaning of the opposition remains.

9 Boege, *Los mazatecos ante la nación*, p. 143.

18

Ziryab

For Julieta Aréchiga and Héctor Palacios

The lute, the voice of the Bedouin *dawar* (encampment), was born from the cooing of doves. When the lute sang in palace pavilions, it blended with the poems of female slaves. Because its belly bulged, its sounds spun inside it, came out to merge with the cadence of the poems, surrounded the fountains in the garden, gyrated next to the sandalwood's perfume, and knew how to envelop lovers. Its sounds, drowsy now with the rustle of silk and the warmth of bodies, settled in the darkest of circles under eyes.

The guitar, the cry of the Moorish festival, was born from the rooster's crowing. During the festival, it learned to reflect the vibrations of its chords on the flat bottom of its box and then shoot its notes into the wind like arrows. Its melodies and its singers' voices were arrows. They flew directly through the air, ripped through the branches of the myrtle trees, called people to pleasure, and soared on freely to the most remote places to drive the turtle doves from their watering spots or to imbed themselves on the face of the moon.

The guitar's name (in Spanish, *guitarra*) emphasizes the final open vowel. The lute's name (in Spanish *laúd*) is dissolved in a final loop.

Strumming and picking. The lute builds the melody. Soon, from the background, the guitar's notes rise slowly to firmly cover the lute's sweet sound. I hear a record by Paco de Lucía. The tune is the name of the record—Zyryab—written that way, with two *y*s. The record's notes explain that Ziryab, a musician from Baghdad who lived at the court of 'Abd-al-Rahmán II, is considered to be the inventor of the guitar because he added a fifth string to the lute's four. Ziryab was famed for establishing a school of music in Córdoba, and he was greatly influential in the development of Andalucian-Arabian music.

Was Ziryab, as the pamphlet said, the guitar's inventor? It is perhaps better to consider him to be a great innovator in the long evolution of musical instruments. In effect, Ziryab added one more string to the four-stringed lute, changed the plectrum from wood to an eagle's claw, increased the number of frets from four to six, and substituted lion intestine for silk in the strings.

Abu-l-Hasán, Alí ibn Nafi, nicknamed Ziryab (Blackbird) because of his dark skin, was born in Mesopotamia at the end of the eighth century. He was a freed slave who studied with Isahaq-al-Mawsili, one of the most famous musicians at the court of Baghdad. The young student's talent came to the attention of Harun al-Raxid, the famous Abassid caliph of *The Thousand and One Nights,* who asked Isahaq al-Mawsili to bring Ziryab so that he could hear him play. Ziryab's success before the caliph made his teacher jealous, and the young musician became the target of so many palace intrigues that he had to renounce his career at the court and ask for protection in distant lands. Ziryab left Baghdad, went to other courts, and finally sailed to the West. In 822 he arrived in Córdoba at the court of the city's emir, 'Abd al-Rahmán II.

Ziryab was well received in Córdoba. The musician and singer became a model of good taste. Brought up in the elegance and luxury of the caliphate, he exercised considerable influence on the Cordovans with his polished style in dress, etiquette, cuisine, and furniture. Among other things, he taught his admirers that the colors of clothing should change with each season, as they did in Baghdad. As might be expected, his greatest influence was in the area of music and song. The times were propitious for him in Córdoba, because during the reign of al-Hakan, 'Abd al-Rahmán II's father, Arabian music, of mixed Bedouin and Greek-Persian origin, had been introduced in al-Andalus (Spain) by musicians and slave singers whom the emir brought to the court from the East. Ziryab had his own chorus of slave singers at the emir's court, and at the conservatory he taught everything from the ten tonalities of music according to Ptolemy to a vast repertory of Arabian songs.

Ziryab was over sixty when he died in   857, leaving, among other things, his legacy of the lute's fifth string.

The fifth string was red. It repeated the second string's color, and it was placed between the second string and the third. It represented breathing. It gave a finer quality to the lute and made it more effective, because respiration, in Arabian thought, was not only a current of air but also a vital breath, the bridge between the soul and the body.

Ziryab had to take all of this into account. He could not violate a law of nature by introducing a strange element without justification. The four original colors of the lute agreed with the body's four humors, and in turn with the four elements, according to the well-known philosophical principles the Arabs had inherited from the Greeks. Red was for blood, and blood corresponded to air; yellow was for yellow bile, and that corresponded to fire; white was for phlegm, and that corresponded to water; black was for melancholy (black bile), and that corresponded to earth.

He also had to take into account the combination of humors, two by two, to find natural impulses. Arabian medicine taught that blood and phlegm together caused dissolution; phlegm and melancholy, contraction; melancholy and yellow bile, coagulation; yellow bile and blood, expansion. In their turn, the natural impulses were applied to the psyche: dissolution liquefied the soul and led to the absorption of all kinds of concepts; contraction caused fear and anguish; coagulation made the soul cling to a single concept; and expansion brought pleasure and joy. The equilibrium of the lute's chords restored the bodily humors. Because of that, music was a therapeutic resource in Arabian medicine.

What a great number of currents of thought the Mediterranean brought together! In Greek mythology, Hermes invented the lyre with three strings, according to some, because there were three seasons, or, according to others, with four, because the year had four trimesters. Apollo increased the strings on the lyre to seven, which corresponded to the seven vowels in the alphabet, and the order of the strings and vowels was used as therapeutic music in the sun god's temples. Musical harmony also reigned in Egypt. The Egyptian priests' songs made a strong impression on listeners because of the sequence of the seven vowels sung with precise musical values.

Old pre-Islamic traditions from the Arabian deserts also came together in the Mediterranean. Very little is known about their persistence; Islam tried to erase all memory of polytheism. But some Arabian gods infiltrated oral literature through fantastic stories. The four wise kings, inhabitants of the horizon from the ends of the earth, were perhaps echoes of a remote cosmic order: al-Abyad, the white king, al-Ahmar, the igneous red king, al-Aswad, the black king, and al-Azraq, the blue king.

Music, numbers, elements, order, spaces, times, colors—fundamental cosmic laws that appear, suggestively, throughout the width and breadth of the planet.

It is common in Mesoamerican traditions to find that the four colors associated with the quadrants of the earth's surface were symbols of an order that governed the entire universe. In Mesoamerica, the four colors represented the correspondence between times and spaces, and they designated the places through which time flowed. At the ends of the world, four trees held up the skies, and the divine forces that came from on high and from below flowed inside their trunks. The colors might vary, and it is possible that besides the four colors at the ends of the world there was a fifth color, that of the central tree, the axis of the universe. But in the codices, in songs, and in narrations the symbolism of color was always important.

And music? What value did music have in Mesoamerica's mythical concepts? How was music associated with the order of times and spaces in the complex of four colors? The ancient Nahua had a myth in which the symbols of the great order included celestial musicians as characters. The myth is found in two sources from the sixteenth century. The document called *Historia de México* gives the following text:

They also say that this same god [Tezcatlipuca] created the air, which appeared as a black figure, with a great thorn covered with blood, the sign of sacrifice. And Tezcatlipuca said to the figure, "Wind, go across the sea to the house of the Sun, who has many musicians and trumpeters there, who serve him and sing. Among them is one with three feet, and the others have such big ears they cover the whole body. Once you have arrived at the shore, you will call my servants Acapachtli, that is "turtle," and Acihuatl, who is "half woman, half fish," and Atlicipactli, who is the "whale," and you will tell them to make a bridge so you can cross over, and you will bring the musicians with their instruments from the house of the Sun to do me honor. And saying this, he departed and was never seen again.

Then the god of the air went to the seashore and called their names; and they came hastily and made a bridge, over which he crossed. The Sun, seeing him coming, said to the musicians, "Here is the miserable one. Let no one answer, because anyone who answers will go with him."

These musicians were dressed in the four colors: white, red, yellow, and green.

Then the god of air, having arrived, called them with song. One of them answered immediately, and went with him and took the music, which is what they now use in their dances in honor of their gods.[1]

The second source for the myth is the *Historia eclesiástica indiana* by Friar Gerónimo Mendieta. The text reads:

How Tezcatlipoca appeared to one of his worshippers and sent him to the house of the Sun

Humans who had worshipped those dead gods who had left them their mantles as remembrances were said to be walking around sad and pensive, each one wrapped in a mantle, looking and searching to see if they could see their gods or if they would appear. They say that one of the devotees of Tezcatlipoca (who was the principal god of México), persevering in his devotion, came to the seacoast, where three forms or figures appeared, and they called to him and said, "Come here, so-and-so, you are such a friend of mine that I want you to go to the house of the Sun and bring singers and instruments from there so that you can make a feast for me. In order for you to do so, you will call the whale, the siren and the turtle, who will make a bridge that will allow you to cross over." Once the bridge was made, and after singing his song, the Sun heard it, and told his people and servants not to answer the song because whoever did so would be taken away. And it happened that some of them, thinking that the song was melodious, answered him and he brought them with the drum they call *huehuetl,* and with the *tepunaztli.* They say that with those they began to have feasts and dances for their gods, and that the songs that the

[1] *Historia de México,* pp. 111–12.

singers sang at those festivals were considered to be prayers, performing them in the same tone and movements and with such good sense and judgment that they did not miss a single note or a step. That same arrangement is followed today. However, it goes without saying that they are not to be allowed to sing the ancient songs, because all of them are full of idolatrous memories or of diabolic or suspicious symbols, which amount to the same thing.[2]

Let us study the meaning of the myth, concentrating on the significant part. There were two characters who represented the two halves of the universe. One, Tezcatlipoca, was the god of darkness. The other, the sun, was warm and celestial. Tezcatlipoca had the assistance of his agent and creature Ehecatl, the wind god, cold like himself, black, shadowy, and armed with a bloody thorn. The sun, on the other hand, had an orchestra composed of musicians dressed in four colors.

Tezcatlipoca's dark son had the mission of trapping the musicians with his melodious song. The sons of the sun had the obligation to ignore the dark, cold, nocturnal call. What did Tezcatlipoca propose to do? He wanted to begin the fight, the alternation of the two opposites. The sun, in turn, wanted to keep the light of his sons pure. He didn't want it to alternate with the wind's blackness and coldness. But the world had to begin its course, and destiny had to be fulfilled. The song's strength was greater than the musicians' resistance, and one by one they were captured so that the dances and feasts could begin on earth.

The mention of the four colors indicates the distribution of the musicians at the four corners of the universe. The lord of night's successive conquest of each of the sun's servants shows the way in which each unit of time emerged in its turn from one of the four corners of the world by way of one of the cosmic trees. Time was the union of the opposing forces—the luminous

2 Mendieta, *Historia eclesiástica indiana,* vol. 1, book 2, chapter 3, p. 86.

and the obscure, the colorful and the black, the day and the night, the dry and the wet. The alternation and the cycles were established. The dance and the feast were thus changed into symbols of the gyration of the gods, converted into time. They represented the existence on the earth's surface of a motion that created all the realities of history.

Human expression of beauty was made the equivalent of the supreme beauty of the gods—the geometric order of movement. Dance, the maximum fusion of the divine and the human, is the gyration of colors that follow the command of the musical instruments.

References Cited

Abbreviations

AGN	Archivo General de la Nación
FCE	Fondo de Cultura Económica
IIA	Instituto de Investigaciones Antropológicas
IH	Instituto de Historia
IIH	Instituto de Investigaciones Históricas
III	Instituto Indigenista Interamericano
INAH	Instituto Nacional de Antropología e Historia
INI	Instituto Nacional Indigenista
MAMH	Memoria Academia Mexicana de Historia
SEP	Secretaría de Educación Pública
SG	Secretaría de Gobernación
SHCP	Secretaría de Hacienda y Crédito Público
SMA	Sociedad Mexicana de Antropología
UAM	Universidad Autónoma Metropolitana
UACH	Universidad Autónoma de Chiapas
UNAM	Universidad Nacional Autónoma de México

Anales de Cuauhtitlán. 1945. In *Códice Chimalpopoca,* pp. 1–118, 145–64. P. F. Velázquez, trans. Mexico City: UNAM-IH.

Aramoni Burguete, M. E. 1990. *Talokan Tata, Talokan Nana: Hierofanías y testimonios de un mundo indígena.* Mexico City: Consejo Nacional para la Cultura y las Artes.

Boege, E. 1988. *Los mazatecos ante la nación: Contradicciones de la identidad étnica en el México actual.* Mexico City: Siglo Veintiuno Editores.

Book of Chilam Balam of Chumayel. 1967. R. L. Roys, trans. Norman: University of Oklahoma Press.

Bourdieu, P. 1977. *An Outline of a Theory of Practice*. Cambridge: Cambridge Univ. Press.

Cárdenas, J. de. 1980 [1591]. *Problemas y secretos maravillosos de las Indias*. 5th. ed. X. Lozoya, ed. Mexico City: Academia Nacional de Medicina.

Carias, C. M., H. M. Leyva, R. Martínez Miralda, E. L. Ordóñez S., and J. F. Travieso. 1988. *Tradición oral indígena de Yamaranguila*. Tegucigalpa: Guaymuras.

Carrasco, P. 1971. "La importancia de las sobrevivencias prehispánicas en la religión tarasca: La lluvia." *Verhandlungen des 38 Internationalen Amerikanistenkongresses, Stuttgart-München*. vol. 3, pp. 265–75.

Carrasco, P., and R. J. Weitlaner. 1952. "El Sol y la Luna." *Tlalocan* 3 (2): 168–74.

Caso, A. 1942. "El aguila y el nopal." MAMH 5 (2): 93–104.

Chimalpahin Cuauhtlehuanitzin, F. de S. A. M. 1965. *Relaciones originales de Chalco Amaquemecan*. S. Rendón, trans. Mexico City: FCE.

Chronicles of Michoacán. 1970. E. R. Craine and R. C. Reindorp, eds. and trans. Norman: University of Oklahoma Press.

Codex Borbonicus. 1974. K. A. Nowotny and J. de Durand-Forest, eds. Graz: Akademische Druck (facsimile).

Codex Borgia. 1963. Mexico City: FCE (facsimile).

Codex Mendoza. 1992. F. F. Berdan and P. R. Anawalt, eds. Berkeley: University of California Press.

Códice Florentino: Manuscrito 218-20 de la Colección Palatina de la Biblioteca Medicea Laurenziana. 1979. 3 vols. Mexico City: SG/AGN (facsimile).

Códice Telleriano-Remensis. 1964–1967. In Lord Kingsborough, *Antigüedades de México*, vol. 1., pp. 151–338. J. Corona Núñez, ed. Mexico City: SHCP (facsimile).

Códice Vaticano Latino 3738, or *Códice Vaticano Ríos*, or *Códice Ríos*. 1964–1967. In Lord Kingsborough, *Antigüedades de México*. vol. 3., pp. 7–314. J. Corona Nuñez, ed. Mexico City: SHCP (facsimile).

Códice Vindobonensis, or *Códice de Viena*, or *Mexicanus 1*. 1964–1967. In Lord Kingsborough, *Antigüedades de México*. vol. 4, pp.

4, 51–184. J. Corona Núñez, ed. Mexico City: SHCP (facsimile).

Colmenero de Ledesma, A. 1652 [1631]. *Chocolate, or, an Indian drink, by the wise and moderate use whereof, health is preserved* . . . Translation of *Curioso tratado de la naturaleza y calidad del chocolate.* J. Wadsworth, trans. London: John Dakins.

Durán, Fr. D. 1994. *The History of the Indies of New Spain.* D. Heyden, trans. Norman: University of Oklahoma Press.

Epic of Gilgamesh. 1985. M. G. Kovacs, trans. and ed. Stanford, California: Stanford University Press.

Evans-Pritchard, E. E. 1973. "Foreword." In R. Needham, ed., *Right and Left: Essays on Dual Symbolic Classification.* Chicago: University of Chicago Press.

Fernández de Oviedo y Valdés, G. 1944–1945. *Historia general y natural de las Indias, islas y tierra-firme del mar océano.* 14 vols. J. Amador de los Ríos, ed. Asunción, Paraguay: Editorial Guaranía.

Florentine Codex. 1950–1982. 12 books. A. J. O. Anderson and C. E. Dibble, eds. and trans. Salt Lake City: University of Utah Press.

Foster, G. M. 1978. "Hippocrates' Latin American Legacy: 'Hot' and 'Cold' in Contemporary Folk Medicine." In R. K. Wetherington, ed., *Colloquia in Anthropology.* vol. 2, pp. 3–19. Dallas, Texas: Southern Methodist University, Fort Burgwin Research Center.

Frazer, J. 1959. *The New Golden Bough.* New York: Mentor.

Fuentes y Guzmán, F. A. 1932–1933. *Recordación florida: Discurso historial y demostración* . . . 3 vols. Guatemala: Sociedad de Geografía e Historia.

Furst, P. 1972. "Para encontrar nuestra vida: El peyote entre los huicholes." In S. Nahmad, O. Klineberg, P. Furst, and B. Myerhoff, *El peyote y los huicholes,* pp. 109–91. Mexico City: SEP (SEP/Setentas: 29).

Galinier, J. 1987. *Pueblos de la Sierra Madre: Etnografía de la comunidad otomí.* M. Sánchez Ventura and P. Chéron, trans. Mexico City: INI/Centre d'Etudes Mexicaines et Centramericaines.

Girón Gómez, J. 1989. "El Sol y la Luna." In M. Encino Gómez et al., *Cuentos y relatos indígenas,* pp. 35–40. Mexico City: UNAM.

Gossen, G. H. 1979. *Los chamulas en el mundo del sol*. C. Paschero, trans. Mexico City: INI.

Graulich, M. 1990. *Mitos y rituales del México antiguo*. A. Barral Gómez, trans. Madrid: Colegio Universitario/Ediciones Istmo.

Graves, R. 1960. *The Greek Myths*. Hammondsworth: Penguin.

Guil'liem Arroyo, S. 1989. "Descubrimiento de una pintura mural en Tlatelolco." *Antropológicas* (UNAM) no. 3, pp. 145–50.

Guiteras Holmes, C. 1965. *Los peligros del alma: Visión del mundo de un tzotzil*. C. A. Castro, trans. Mexico City: FCE.

Hermitte, M. E. 1970. *Poder sobrenatural y control social*. C. Viqueira, trans. Mexico City: III.

Hernández, F. 1959. *Historia natural de Nueva España*. J. Rojo Navarro, trans. In Francisco Hernández, *Obras completas*. vols. 2, 3. Mexico City: UNAM.

Hertz, R. 1973. "The Pre-eminence of the Right Hand: A Study in Religious Polarity." In R. Needham, ed., *Right and Left: Essays on Dual Symbolic Classification*, pp. 3–31. Chicago: University of Chicago Press.

Historia de los mexicanos por sus pinturas. 1965. In A. Ma. Garibay K., ed., *Teogonía e historia de los mexicanos: Tres opúsculos del siglo XVI*, pp. 21–90. Mexico City: Editorial Porrúa.

Historia de México (Histoire du Mechique). 1965. R. Rosales Munguía, trans. In A. Ma. Garibay K., ed., *Teogonía e historia de los mexicanos: Tres opúsculos del siglo XVI*, pp. 91–120. Mexico City: Editorial Porrúa.

Hollembach, E. E. de. 1980. "El mundo animal en el folklore de los triques de Copala." *Tlalocan* 8: 437–90.

Ichon, A. 1973. *La religión de los totonacas de la sierra*. J. Arenas, trans. Mexico City: INI.

Jansen, M. E. R. G. N. 1982. *Huisi tacu: Estudio interpretativo de un libro mixteco antiguo, Codex Vindobonensis Mexicanus I*. 2 vols. Amsterdam: Centro de Estudios y Documentación Latinoamericanos.

Kirchhoff, P. 1960. *Mesoamérica: Sus límites geográficos, composición étnica y carácteres culturales*. 2d ed. *Revista Tlatoani (México)* Supplement no. 3.

Koran. 1978. 4th. ed. A. Lane, trans. London: Penguin Books.

Krickeberg, Walter. 1969. *Feldsbilder Mexicos.* Berlin: Dietrich Reimer.

Landa, Fr. D. de. 1982. *Relación de las cosas de Yucatán.* 12th ed. Mexico City: Editorial Porrúa.

Las Casas, Fr. B. de. 1967. *Apologética historia sumaria.* 2 vols. E. O'Gorman, ed. Mexico City: UNAM-IIH.

León, N. 1968. "¿Cual era el nombre gentilicio de los tarascos y el origen de este último?" *Anales del Museo Michoacano,* pp. 29–32. Guadalajara: Edmundo Aviña Levy (facsimile).

Leyenda de los soles. 1945. In *Códice Chimalpopoca,* pp. 119–64. P. F. Velázquez, trans. Mexico City: UNAM-IH.

Lok, R. 1987. "The House as Microcosm: Some Cosmic Representations in a Mexican Indian Village." In R. de Ridder and J. A. J. Karremans, eds., *The Leiden Tradition in Structural Anthropology: Essays in Honour of P. E. de Josselin de Jong,* pp. 211–23. Leiden: Brill.

López Austin, A. 1972. "El mal aire en el México prehispánico." *Religión en Mesoamérica,* pp. 399–408. 12th Mesa Redonda. Mexico City: SMA.

———. 1973. *Hombre-dios: Religión y política en el mundo náhuatl.* Mexico City: UNAM-IIH.

———. 1981. *Tarascas y mexicas.* Mexico City: FCE/SEP.

———. 1988. *Human Body and Ideology: Concepts of the Ancient Nahuas.* 2 vols. T. Ortiz de Montellano and B. R. Ortiz de Montellano, trans. Salt Lake City: University of Utah Press.

———. 1993. *Myths of the Opossum: Pathways of Mesoamerican Mythology.* B. R. Ortiz de Montellano and T. Ortiz de Montellano, trans. Albuquerque: University of New Mexico Press.

López Gómez, M. 1989. "La formación del cielo, del sol y la luna, y la maldición del Anticristo, el maíz." In M. Encino Gómez et al., *Cuentos y relatos indígenas,* pp. 93–118. Mexico City: UNAM.

López Luján, L. 1994. *The Offerings of the Templo Mayor of Tenochtitlan.* B. R. Ortiz de Montellano and T. Ortiz de Montellano, trans. Boulder: University Press of Colorado.

Madsen, W. 1955. "Hot and Cold in the Universe of San Francisco Tecospa, Valley of Mexico." *Journal of American Folklore* 68: 123–39.
———. 1960. *The Virgin's Children: Life in an Aztec Village Today.*
Austin: University of Texas Press.

Mendieta, Fr. G. de. 1954. *Historia eclesiástica indiana.* 4 vols. Mexico
City: Salvador Chávez Hayhoe.

Miller, W. S. 1956. *Cuentos mixes.* Mexico City: INI.

Morales Bermúdez, J. 1984. *On o t'ian: Narrativa indígena chol.* Mexico
City: UAM-Azcapotzalco.

Motolinía, Fr. T. de. 1971 [1540]. *Memoriales.* E. O'Gorman, ed. Mexico City: UNAM.

Needham, R., ed. 1973. *Right and Left: Essays on Dual Symbolic Classification.* Chicago: University of Chicago Press.

Neuenswander, H. 1981. "Vestiges of Early Maya Time Concepts in a
Contemporary Maya (Cubulco Achi) Community: Implications for Epigraphy." *Estudios de Cultura Maya* 13: 125–63.

New American Bible. 1970. Encino, California: Benziger.

Ortiz de Montellano, B. R. 1990. *Aztec Medicine, Health, and Nutrition.*
New Brunswick: Rutgers University Press.

Petrich, P. 1985. *La alimentación mochó: Acto y palabra (Estudio etno-
lingüístico).* San Cristóbal de las Casas: Centro de Estudios Indígenas, UACH.

Portal, M. A. 1986. *Cuentos y mitos en una zona mazateca.* Mexico City:
INAH.

Preuss, K. T. 1982. *Mitos y cuentos nahuas de la Sierra Madre Occidental.* E.
Ziehm, ed., M. Frenk-Westheim, trans. Mexico City: INI.

Redfield, M. P. 1935. *The Folk Literature of a Yucatecan Town.* Washington, D.C.: Carnegie Institution.

*Relación de las ceremonias y ritos y población y gobierno de los indios de la
provincia de Michoacán (1541).* 1977. J. Tudela, ed. Morelia, Michoacán: Balsal Editores (facsimile).

Relatos, mitos y leyendas de la Chinantla. 1981. 2d ed. R. L. Weitlaner,
ed. Mexico City: INI.

Ruiz de Alarcón, H. 1953 [1629]. *Tratado de las idolatrías, supersticiones,
dioses, ritos, hechizerías y otras costumbres gentílicas de las razas
aborígenes.* Mexico City: Ediciones Fuente Cultural.

————. 1982 [1629]. *Aztec Sorcerers in Seventeenth Century Mexico City: The Treatise on Superstitions by Hernando Ruiz de Alarcón.* M. D. Coe and C. Whittaker, eds. and trans. Albany: State University of New York, Institute of Mesoamerican Studies.

————. 1984 [1629]. *Treatise on the Heathen Superstitions.* J. R. Andrews and R. Hassig, eds. and trans. Norman: University of Oklahoma Press.

Sahagún, Fr. B. de. 1979. *Códice Florentino: Manuscrito 218-20 de la Colección Palatina de la Biblioteca Medicea Laurenziana.* 3 vols. Mexico City: AGN/Secretaría de Gobernación (facsimile).

————. 1989. *Historia general de las cosas de Nueva España.* 2 vols. A. López Austin and J. García Quintana, introduction, glossary, and notes. Mexico City: CNCA/Alianza Editorial Mexicana.

————. *Primeros memoriales* (Nahuatl texts of Sahagún's informants). 1993. F. Anders, ed. Norman: University of Oklahoma Press (facsimile).

Santamaría, F. J. 1974. *Diccionario de mejicanismos.* 2d ed. Mexico City: Editorial Porrúa.

Schele, L., and M. L. Miller. 1986. *The Blood of Kings.* New York: George Braziller.

Segre, E. 1990. *Metamorfosis de lo sagrado y de lo profano: Narrativa náhuat de la Sierra Norte de Puebla.* Mexico City: INAH.

Seler, E. 1904. Wall paintings of Mitla. In Eduard Seler et al., *Mexican and Central American Antiquities: Calendar Systems, and History,* pp. 243–324. C. P. Bowditch, trans. Washington, D. C.: Smithsonian Institution.

Siméon, R. 1977. *Diccionario de la lengua náhuatl o mexicana.* J. Oliva de Coll, trans. Mexico City: Siglo Veintiuno Editores.

Suárez de Cepeda, J. 1983 [1581]. *Relación de los indios colimas de la Nueva Granada.* Mexico City: Innovación.

Taggart, J. M. 1983. *Nahuat Myth and Social Structure.* Austin: University of Texas Press.

Torquemada, Fr. J. de. 1969. *Monarquía indiana.* 3 vols. 4th ed. Mexico City: Editorial Porrúa.

van Zantwijk, R., R. de Ridder, and E. Braakhuis, eds. 1990. *Mesoamerican Dualism/Dualismo mesoamericano.* Utrecht: RUU-ISOR.

Veytia, M. 1944. *Historia antigua de México.* 2 vols. Mexico City: Editorial Leyenda.

Vogt, E. Z. 1983. *Ofrendas para los dioses: Análisis simbólico de rituales zinacantecos.* Mexico City: FCE.

Weitlaner, R. J., and C. A. Castro. 1973. *Usila (morada de colibríes).* Mexico City: Museo Nacional de Antropología.

Whitecotton, J. W. 1977. *The Zapotec. Princes, Priests, and Peasants.* Norman: University of Oklahoma Press.

Translators' Note

The following essays were originally published in *México Indígena:*

"El conejo en la cara de la luna," number 12, September 1990
"Mitos y nombres," number 13, October 1990
"El invento y el descubrimiento en la concepción mítica del mundo,"
number 14, November 1990
"El barro," number 15, December 1990
"Las palabras del conjuro," numbers 16–17, January–February 1991
"El mito en la tradición religiosa mesoamericana," number 18, March
1991
"Los dichos," number 19, April 1991
"Fruto asombroso," number 20, May 1991
"El milagro del águila y el nopal," number 21, June 1991
"El eclipse," number 22, July 1991
"El anticristo y los soles," number 23, August 1991
"Relatos de tlacuaches," number 24, September 1991

The following essays were originally published in *Ojarascas:*

"El nombre de los tarascos," number 1, October 1991
"Nuestros primeros padres," number 2, November 1991
"La mano derecha, la mano izquierda," numbers 3–4, December 1991,
January 1992
"Complementos y composiciones," number 5, February 1992
"Sinonimias," number 6, March 1992
"Ziryab," number 7, April 1992

Index

INDEX